D1243404

WE BELIEVE

A Prayer Book
Based on the Augsburg Confession

Richard F. Bansemer

Reflections by
Walter R. Bouman

The American Lutheran Publicity Bureau

© 1999 by The American Lutheran Publicity Bureau
P.O. Box 327, Delhi, New York 13753-0327
All rights reserved

Printed in the United States of America
ISBN 1-892921-00-6

To the people of the Virginia Synod,
and to our companion synod,
The Island's District of Papua New Guinea,
brothers and sisters in Christ.

CONTENTS

Part II Articles About Matters in Dispute*

*Note: Articles 22–28 are articles dealing with matters of dispute in the 16th century. Most of the articles are necessarily abbreviated. Translated excerpts are from the original German text of the Augsburg Confession, except in a few cases where use of translation from the original Latin made it possible to be more concise.

INTRODUCTION

This book seeks to use the Augsburg Confession devotionally, in order that theology and prayer may enliven faith.

The Augsburg Confession has 28 articles divided in two parts. Articles 1–21 are basic articles of faith. Articles 22–28 are "Articles About Matters in Dispute ... Which Have Been Corrected," and may not be as pertinent to our time as they were in 1530 when they were written. However, prayers and reflections are provided for all 28 articles, making the long teaching season of Pentecost (one per Sunday) ideal for their use, either in Sunday worship or at other teaching opportunities.

Three types of prayers are offered for each of the 28 articles included here:

(1) A collect is available for each article for use in public or private worship. The season of Pentecost may be an appropriate time to use these prayers publicly.

(2) A main prayer for congregational use is also provided.

(3) Additionally, personal prayers are provided for those who wish to pray the themes of the confessions privately.

Preceding each set of prayers, a Scripture text and reflection have been provided by the Rev. Dr. Walter R. Bouman of Trinity Lutheran Seminary, Columbus, Ohio. It is an honor for me to have someone as recognized as Dr. Bouman make such a major contribution to this book. His scholarship and ecumenical spirit are known throughout the Lutheran Church in North America, the Episcopal Church, and beyond.

Confessional churches of all denominations understand that it is not sufficient to simply "do theology" at the whim of a particular society. Rather, revealed truth and doctrine are constant, and the power and need of the cross of Christ never diminish.

I am indebted to the Virginia Synod of the Evangelical Lutheran Church in America, which provided sabbatical time to work on these prayers, and to my colleague, Pastor Jim Mauney, who suggested using the Lutheran confessions as a prayer resource.

Finally, I again thank Connie Seddon of the American Lutheran Publicity Bureau for her meticulous editing and personal support.

PART I

Articles of Faith
and Doctrine

ARTICLE 1

God

We unanimously hold and teach, in accordance with the decree of the Council of Nicaea, that there is one divine essence, which is called and which is truly God, and that there are three persons in this one divine essence, equal in power and alike eternal: God the Father, God the Son, God the Holy Spirit. All three persons are one divine essence, eternal, without division, without end, of infinite power, wisdom, and goodness, one creator and preserver of all things visible and invisible.

A Reading from the New Testament

For all who are led by the Spirit of God are children of God. For you did not receive a spirit of slavery to fall back into fear, but you have received a spirit of adoption. When we cry, "Abba! Father!" it is that very Spirit bearing witness with our spirit that we are children of God, and if children, then heirs, heirs of God and joint heirs with Christ—if, in fact, we suffer with him so that we may also be glorified with him (Romans 8:14–17).

Reflection

Our Reformation ancestors began with a confession of the Triune God, not because confession of the Trinity was a legal requirement in the empire, but because the doctrine of the Trinity is a doctrine of the Gospel. The Bible does not have a "doctrine" of the Trinity, but its story requires us to confess God as Trinity. Martin Luther taught the church to think once again of God as a suffering God, a vulnerable God. The Gospel of the crucified God tells us that the Son dies, the Father grieves, and the Holy Spirit witnesses that this suffering is *for you.*

The great and final freedom of God is not the freedom of autonomy, the freedom of noninvolvement, the freedom *from* something. It is rather the freedom of love, the freedom of relationship, the freedom *for* something. God's freedom is to be *for* the world, to be involved with the world. The freedom of love is vulnerable, capable of suffering for the beloved.

Thus the confession of the Triune God is a doctrine of great comfort. The Triune God is not distant or apathetic, but rather very close to us. There is no place so lonely, no situation so hopeless, no feeling so abandoned that God does not embrace and encompass it. Because God's suffering belongs to the Gospel, we know that suffering does not have the last word. The Gospel is the story of the victorious love of God. "No, in all these things we are more than conquerors through him who loved us. For I am convinced that neither death, nor life, nor angels, nor rulers, nor things present, nor things to come, nor powers, nor height, nor depth, nor anything else in all creation, will be able to separate us from the love of God in Christ Jesus our Lord" (Romans 8:37–39).

Collect
God, you are named Father, Son, and Holy Spirit, names of lowliness, names of the earth. As you live with us here, as well as in heaven, you still create from the dust, preserve with your Spirit, and fill us with your presence through Jesus Christ, our Lord. For your goodness, love, wisdom, and companionship, receive our thanks, now and forever. Amen.

Congregational Prayer
Heavenly Father, you are the "I AM" God, being whatever pleases you, doing goodness for all time. We come before you as your created ones, made in your image, that we might reflect godly qualities through our lives. We thank you for your Spirit, holy and eternal, which will not depart from us, and for your Son, Jesus Christ, our teacher and our redeemer.

God Almighty, thank you for telling us about yourself. Without your revelation, we would fashion you in our own image, after our own likeness, or make you so far away and unreachable that we would worship you from fear and ignorance, as pagans do.

We come to you in prayer to know you better as person. We come to you with loneliness. All of our emptiness fills us with both a dread of today's events and a need of your companionship. Come, live among us still, and continue to teach us your ways.

We come to you in selfishness, aware that we take very good care of ourselves, but do not see our neighbor as your daughter or son, our sister or brother. We come to you that we may be lovers of justice, willing to share the bounty you bestow upon us all.

We come to you in deep need, afraid of disease and dying, unable to comprehend time before us or life eternal. We ask that you would fill us with faith beyond understanding, knowing how mere knowledge is weak without you. Give us faith, we ask, and when we sense its presence, give us the wisdom to thank you for it. Amen.

Personal Prayer

God of the visible, I come with my problems and pains, my fears and disloyalties, my aging sin-sick body and my desire for immortality. Some of what I come with is selfish and weak. Some is very misguided, but all is placed before you to sort and sift, and to respond.

God of the invisible, I come with the senses of the earth—with sight and sound, with touch, taste, and smell—to learn of your invisible world beyond this time and place. I come with the wrong senses, and often with the wrong motivations. I know that I have not settled all matters in this world of the physical, but because you tell of an invisible world, my invisible sin-sick soul yearns for a better place.

God of the visible and invisible, I feel like a lost stranger in both worlds. In the physical world, I am not content, because I am estranged from you and others. In the invisible world, my faith is too weak to discern it as a world to come, a world that has been, or a world here and now.

Father, Son, and Holy Spirit, mystery divine, touch my personal life with your personal touch, that I may be filled with faith in the yet-to-be-seen. Show me your faithfulness that I may have courage. Tell me your story that I may give thanks. Feed me with your gifts of bread and wine that I may know I've been part and parcel of all your worlds.

For giving me life, thank you. For hope and expectation of more to come, thank you. For joys unseen and worlds unexplored, receive my heart and soul, an invisible offering for your purpose. Amen.

ARTICLE 2

Original Sin

It is also taught among us that since the fall of Adam all men who are born according to the course of nature are conceived and born in sin. That is, all men are full of evil lust and inclinations from their mothers' wombs and are unable by nature to have true fear of God and true faith in God. Moreover, this inborn sickness and hereditary sin is truly sin and condemns to the eternal wrath of God all those who are not born again through Baptism and the Holy Spirit.

A Reading from the New Testament

Ever since the creation of the world [God's] eternal power and divine nature, invisible though they are, have been understood and seen through the things he has made. So they are without excuse; for though they knew God, they did not honor him as God or give thanks to him, but they became futile in their thinking, and their senseless minds were darkened. Claiming to be wise, they became fools; and they exchanged the glory of the immortal God for images resembling a mortal human being or birds or four-footed animals or reptiles (Romans 1:20–23).

Reflection

"Everything is known more profoundly, known for what it really is, in the light of the Gospel. Because of the Gospel the church recognizes both the power and the reality of sin. Because sin is fundamentally a theological reality, because it is against God and the [kingdom] of God, therefore it is not adequately recognized and confessed apart from the Gospel....

"Humanity is alienated from the [kingdom] of God, from God's call and vision for us as creation. Humanity has fallen from the freedom for love [into] the bondage of self-absorption or self-hatred. Humanity has fallen prey to the reign of death. The powers that serve death drive us to self-protection at whatever cost to others or to self-hatred at the cost of distortion of the self. We serve the powers of death also and not least in our driven quest for 'prosperity.'...

"Humanity is captive to false gods, ... religious or secular; or it is captive to equally false autonomy, seeking to be a law unto itself. [Our Reformation ancestors recognized] that in the last analysis sin is not so much misbehavior as it is misbelief. [We do not have 'true fear of God and true faith in God.' This results either in] groundless arrogance or equally groundless despair. Such misbelief or misdirected [trust] means that the whole of our existence, not just individual acts, is guilty existence, existence under condemnation" (Lutheran-Episcopal Dialogue III 1988, 66).

Collect

Heavenly Father, we have to be told by your precious Word that we are by nature sinful and unclean. From our first breath we are far from what you created us to be. We ask you to forgive us our ever present inclination to evil. Birth us again through Baptism and the Holy Spirit that we may be your children forever, for the sake of him who died for us, Jesus Christ our Lord. Amen.

Congregational Prayer

God of mercy, we are reluctant to admit our desperate need of you. Our preoccupation with this life with its joys and problems ignores our hopeless predicament. We do not feel doomed without you. We do not understand the cataclysmic battle being fought over us. Like cattle wandering unaware through a battlefield, we don't know what the noise is all about.

In this world of self-justification, where we pretend to be strong and have no fear, not even the cold reminder of our pending deaths and your day of judgment bother us. We have insulated ourselves with false doctrine and wishful thinking. We no longer believe that the fear of the Lord is the beginning of wisdom, not because perfect love has cast out fear, but because we no longer believe you will return to judge.

We repent this day, and ask you to help us understand that Baptism is no mere sprinkling, but a drowning. Help us understand that forgiveness comes with the high price of the blood of Christ, shed on the cross and shared in the Holy Communion. Give us no peace of mind, until our mind is won by the mind of Christ. Amen.

Personal Prayer

Lord, I hardly know how to confess original sin. I didn't ask to be born, nor to be a sinner. It sounds so universal and condemning. I wonder if it's something I really have to contend with. I easily confess that I am by nature sinful and unclean. There is no sorrow in the admission, just a statement of theological fact.

Lord, I confess that I take your hard work of salvation for granted. I confess that I can grasp neither the depth of Christ's suffering, nor the breadth of his love. I am like a child trying to understand my parents. Help me grow up.

Thank you, Lord, for rescuing me from disaster. Only you could plumb the depths of hell victoriously. Thank you for dying a hard death. I can never forget Calvary. Thank you for paying a price so high, that "body" and "blood" are the only adequate words to describe the cost of my forgiveness in the Holy Communion. Amen.

ARTICLE 3

The Son of God

It is also taught among us that God the Son became man, born of the virgin Mary, and that the two natures, divine and human, are so inseparably united in one person that there is one Christ, true God and true man, who was truly born, suffered, was crucified, died, and was buried in order to be a sacrifice not only for original sin but also for all other sins and to propitiate God's wrath. The same Christ also descended into hell, truly rose from the dead on the third day, ascended into heaven, and sits on the right hand of God, that he may eternally rule and have dominion over all creatures, that through the Holy Spirit he may sanctify, purify, strengthen, and comfort all who believe in him, that he may bestow on them life and every grace and blessing, and that he may protect and defend them against the devil and against sin. The same Lord Christ will return openly to judge the living and the dead, as stated in the Apostles' Creed.

A Reading from the New Testament

Let the same mind be in you that was in Christ Jesus, who, though he was in the form of God, did not regard equality with God as something to be exploited, but emptied himself, taking the form of a slave, being born in human likeness. And being found in human form, he humbled himself and became obedient to the point of death—even death on a cross.

Therefore God also highly exalted him and gave him the name that is above every name, so that at the name of Jesus every knee should bend, in heaven and on earth and under the earth, and every tongue should confess that Jesus Christ is Lord, to the glory of God the Father (Philippians 2:5–11).

Reflection

Our Reformation ancestors made their confession about Jesus, our Lord, with all the classic formulas of the ancient church, especially the great Council of Chalcedon held in A.D. 451. They began with the incarnation, as does the Gospel of John. That is the sequence of history. But sometimes it is helpful to remember that the sequence of recognition is not the same as the sequence of history. How we come to know something is not the same as how it happened. Thus, the Gospel story really begins with its end! It begins with the resurrection of Jesus and his appearances to frightened disciples.

What frightened them was the fear that everything might just be true, that Jesus really is Messiah and

Lord, that in fact human beings had executed the Son of God! When they encountered the risen Jesus they were encountering the One who is beyond death and who therefore has the final power of the future. He is the final judge who has the last word! But just that is the meaning of "God": whoever or whatever has the final power of the future. They worked backwards from there, retrieving everything in the light of this new confession. Jesus' death was the death of God. Jesus' ministry was the presence of God in their midst! Jesus must be the eternal Son of the Father!

In the power of the Holy Spirit they could also envision the future. Death could have no dominion over him. Now they could begin to praise him, pray to him, receive "life and every grace and blessing" from him. The kingdom of God had really begun, and they were in on it.

Collect

Lord Jesus Christ, born of God and Mary, sent from heaven to die for us, through your sacrifice strengthen our faith, comfort our hearts, and forgive us our sins; through your rule protect us against the evil one, and when you return as our judge, look upon us as you looked upon us from the cross—full of mercy. Amen.

Congregational Prayer

Son of God and Son of Mary, divine Lord of all humankind, you left all the joy of heaven behind to come and be with us as teacher, friend, master, and sacrifice. You came and lived the life intended for us from the beginning of time. You showed us by example, and you taught us with the authority of heaven. You forgave us our sins, and instructed us to do likewise to others. You ministered to the sick and the bereaved, the dying and the hungry. You accepted kindness both from the poorest and the richest among us. You told us to pray to our heavenly Father, and you kept sending us out to do the Father's will.

You prayed that we might be one, and you died a miserable death to pay the horrible cost of our estrangement from God. All this you did out of pure love, knowing ahead of time that we had nothing to offer you in return. Accept our praise, not only in this moment of prayer, but in our living of life, that we may reflect your grace, now and forever. Amen.

Personal Prayer

Son of God, you came to earth the human way, wrinkled wet. You brought both pain and joy to your mother Mary.

Son of God, you came to earth for me. You bring both pain and joy. You break apart the life I shouldn't live, so you can be born in me.

Son of God, you came and lived a human life, as raw and real as mine. Now you erase the thought that God the Father doesn't know what my life is like.

Son of God, you send your Holy Spirit to capture my soul. My head is turned around hard. I no longer seek to know myself by looking into a mirror. Your

Spirit shows me the face of God, your face, which brings me joy.

On the day of judgment, come Lord Jesus, filled with mercy. Remember my plight, but most of all, remember your love for me. Amen.

ARTICLE 4

Justification

*It is also taught among us that we cannot obtain
forgiveness of sin and righteousness before God by our
own merits, works, or satisfactions, but that we receive
forgiveness of sin and become righteous before God by
grace, for Christ's sake, through faith, when we believe
that Christ suffered for us and that for his sake our sin is
forgiven and righteousness and eternal life are given to
us. For God will regard and reckon this faith as
righteousness, as Paul says in Romans 3:21–26 and 4:5.*

A Reading from the New Testament
For this reason it depends on faith, in order that the
promise may rest on grace and be guaranteed to all
[Abraham's] descendants, not only to the adherents of
the law but also to those who share the faith of
Abraham (for he is the father of all of us, as it is written,

"I have made you the father of many nations")—in the presence of the God in whom he believed, who gives life to the dead and calls into existence the things that do not exist (Romans 4:16–17).

Reflection

Death threatens the justification of my existence. Therefore I seek to deny my death and thus take charge of my own justification. But that is illusion. I can never be in charge of my ultimate future, and therefore I cannot justify myself.

"The justification of the totality of our existence is disclosed only by the ultimate end of all history. We cannot justify ourselves by means of our efforts or achievements in any sphere because we cannot see, much less determine, the ultimate outcome of history. Indeed, our efforts to justify ourselves in the face of our rebellion against the call to love God and the neighbor are profound expressions of our sinfulness. The Gospel is the proclamation that justification is the gift and promise of God. Jesus of Nazareth, crucified and raised from death for sinners, is both the ground and the hope of the ultimate outcome of history. The meaning of our cosmos and of ourselves is in him (Col. 1:13–20). He is the Alpha and the Omega, the origin and the outcome.

"Trusting him as 'righteousness' and 'justification' means that we are free for our lives and our callings. We have no necessity to use them for justification. We are free to confess sins, to hear the truth of admonition, to experience the grace of God, because the meaningfulness and justification of our lives does not derive from our being in the right. The key term is 'faith' because our justification derives from that event which is promise: Jesus' death and resurrection as God's judgment on our lives and as the outcome of all history" (Lutheran-Episcopal Dialogue III 1988, 93).

Collect
God of grace, increase our faith, that the joys of living our earthly lives your way may free us from the shallow values of the world. Turn our hearts, minds, and wills toward the eternal that is to come, that these brief days may be lived with the expectation of your coming soon. Amen.

Congregational Prayer
God of justice, you make things right according to your own values, for you are God. You have declared that we will be brought into a right relationship with you by grace, as a gift made perfect by your Son, who paid the terrible cost for our forgiveness.

God of justice, we understand the necessity of Jesus' cross. We know we cannot approach you without him. We know that sinners cannot enter into your presence and live. We know that your Son's perfect life is essential for our access to you; we know that his death was a perfect sacrifice, because he was without spot or blemish.

Thank you for Jesus' love of us. Thank you for sending your most precious Son to us. Thank you for loving us as you love him. Amen.

Personal Prayer

Lord Jesus Christ, forgive me for wanting to be the chief agent in my own forgiveness. I want the pleasure of fixing up my own life, without your having to pay any price for me. It is embarrassing to be died for. It is humiliating to think that you would have to die, not just for the whole world, but for me.

No, Lord, I would take the cross away from your history, and out of my life. Your cross means I still need help. Your cross simply won't let me think for a moment that I don't still need you today.

God of justice, you make forgiveness a heavenly matter. You won't let me save myself simply because I cannot save myself. The principalities and powers that your cross defeats are too big for me to imagine, too dangerous for me to approach without you.

Lord Jesus Christ, without my asking, you died for me. You knew I would not like the notion of needing you, but I do need you. Now, give me strength to turn that humbling need into joyful companionship, doing the work you've sent me to do, and being the person you've redeemed for all time. Amen.

ARTICLE 5

The Office of the Ministry

*To obtain such faith God instituted the office of the
ministry, that is, provided the Gospel and the
sacraments. Through these, as through means, he gives
the Holy Spirit, who works faith, when and where he
pleases, in those who hear the Gospel. And the Gospel
teaches that we have a gracious God, not by our own
merits but by the merit of Christ, when we believe this.*

*Condemned are the Anabaptists and others who teach
that the Holy Spirit comes to us through our own
preparations, thoughts, and works without the external
word of the Gospel.*

Readings from the New Testament
When the Advocate comes, whom I will send to you
from the Father, the Spirit of truth who comes from the
Father, he will testify on my behalf. You also are to

testify because you have been with me from the beginning (John 15:26–27).

By contrast, the fruit of the Spirit is love, joy, peace, patience, kindness, generosity, faithfulness, gentleness, and self-control. There is no law against such things. And those who belong to Christ Jesus have crucified the flesh with its passions and desires. If we live by the Spirit, let us also be guided by the Spirit. Let us not become conceited, competing against one another, envying one another (Galatians 5:22–26).

Reflection
The title given to this article long after the Diet (parliament) of Augsburg in 1530 is somewhat misleading. The article is actually about the Holy Spirit. What our Reformation ancestors confessed, and what we want to confess, is that we can know that the Holy Spirit is present whenever a community is animated and shaped by the Gospel and its sacraments.

This is important because the spirits that animate and shape communities are often not the Holy Spirit. Mobs that are driven by the spirit of rage or revenge are led to very destructive actions. There is a spirit there, but it is not the Holy Spirit. Political parties contending for power may have spirit, but not Holy Spirit. Religious enthusiasm may be spirited, but it is related to the Holy Spirit only if it is anchored in the Gospel of Jesus, crucified and risen, and if the fruits somehow match St. Paul's list in Galatians.

Collect

Holy Spirit, come to us this day with the Gospel Word and the Holy Meal to work your great gift of faith in us. Give us what we cannot grasp by our own wills. Give us faith that we may be your people, now and forever. Amen.

Congregational Prayer

Holy Spirit, in your wisdom you have given us pastors and leaders to encourage us in faith, to serve the Holy Meal, and to speak your Word with power.

Gracious God, you provide the Gospel. Graciously you provide teachers of the Gospel, so that what you have done for us may be known to us. Open our ears that faith may begin its holy work in us. Open our hearts, so that we may move beyond understanding to commitment, beyond knowledge to faithful following.

Holy Spirit, we are powerless to believe unless you give us the gift of faith. We are powerless to follow, unless you daily take us by the hand. Do not let us casually drift away from the hearing of your Word. Do not let us avoid you. Hound us with the promises and presence of Christ until we return to you. And when we return, fill us with resolve to wander away no more. Amen.

Personal Prayer

Lord Jesus Christ, I confess to you that I still try to live by the law, in order to have a clear conscience. I still try to save myself by being good. I still harbor thoughts that you will look more kindly upon me on the day of judgment if I can show you how hard I tried.

Jesus, suffering Savior, you died to make me good. You died to take away my sin. You died because you knew the law could not be followed by me, though I try mightily. Help me to understand that when I come to you with nothing in my hands, I come exactly as you want me to come—open, receptive, usable. When I am empty then you can fill me!

Jesus, I know that the law is still there to be followed, but not for the sake of my salvation. That is your work. Yours alone. So save me, dear Lord, until I remember with laughter the days that I tried to save myself. Amen.

The New Obedience

It is also taught among us that such faith should produce good fruits and good works and that we must do all such good works as God has commanded, but we should do them for God's sake and not place our trust in them as if thereby to merit favor before God. For we receive forgiveness of sin and righteousness through faith in Christ, as Christ himself says, "So you also, when you have done all that is commanded you, say, 'We are unworthy servants'" (Luke 17:10). The Fathers also teach thus, for Ambrose says, "It is ordained of God that whoever believes in Christ shall be saved, and he shall have forgiveness of sins, not through works but through faith alone, without merit."

A Reading from the New Testament
For by grace you have been saved through faith, and this is not your own doing; it is the gift of God—not the

result of works, so that no one may boast. For we are what he has made us, created in Christ Jesus for good works, which God prepared beforehand to be our way of life (Ephesians 2:8–10).

Reflection

We Lutherans have learned so well the lesson of the Reformation—justification is by faith and not works—that we are almost afraid to be caught doing good works. But learning just that is not to learn the lesson of the Reformation at all. The Gospel announces that Jesus is risen, that death has no dominion over him, that he is the final power of history. My works, good, bad, or indifferent, do not affect that at all. But when I believe the Gospel, everything changes just because I trust the Gospel. If death does not have the last word, then there is more to do with my life than to preserve it at all costs. Then I am free to offer it in the service of the kingdom of God.

Collect

Heavenly Father, through the offering of Jesus Christ, your good work is known. Now accept the offering of ourselves to his Way and Truth, as our good work of joy and thanksgiving, for the salvation accomplished for us by him.

Congregational Prayer

Lord Jesus Christ, you ask us to do a hard task when you ask us to forgive one another. You know us too well. So often we have come to enjoy our resentments, ill will, and hatreds. You ask us to bury these sins for your sake, for our neighbor's sake, and for our own sake.

Forgiving one another, Lord Jesus, as you forgive us, is what you expect from us, but we are reluctant to obey. We keep holding on to our pride and our pain and our anger. We have been wronged, and we want someone to pay.

Lord Jesus, what a price you paid for us! Your crucifixion is the historical evidence. Your presence with us again today is the current evidence. Your plan for our future together is the most generous evidence of true love. You don't just tolerate us ... you want us! You want us with you. You want us despite our grudges, our pride, our anger, and our weakness.

We do not understand a love this deep, though we receive it. We do not understand what you see in us, but you call us your children anyway.

Lord Jesus, as a thank-you, and only as a thank-you, we forgive one another today, because you ask us to. As a thank-you, we do it, and trust that your gift of peace and new life will follow, for us, and for those who have wronged us. Amen.

Personal Prayer

Lord Jesus, I cannot make faith happen in me. I do not have the power. I am not able to truthfully say that I have more faith in you than in myself.

Lord Jesus, I have invited you to haunt me with your presence, and I have invited you to tell about your love for me over and over again. I have said all the right words. I have even believed in them, if only for a moment, yet my faith is still lacking. I do not live as you would have me live at all times. I am not able to see you in the bad news of my day. I keep expecting you to make me happy.

Lord Jesus, my will is my problem. I want happiness, not you. I want peace, and leisure, and many other good things. When they are missing, I wonder where you are, and I worry about my faith.

Bring me, Jesus Christ, to face the cross without blinking. Bring me, Jesus Christ, to a faith deeper than mellowing-out. Bring me to the God-awful fear that I'm putting my comfort in front of your mission. Bring me, Jesus Christ, to enjoy being your person, even in adversity. Amen.

ARTICLE 7

The Church

It is also taught among us that one holy Christian church will be and remain forever. This is the assembly of all believers among whom the Gospel is preached in its purity and the holy sacraments are administered according to the Gospel. For it is sufficient for the true unity of the Christian church that the Gospel be preached in conformity with a pure understanding of it and the sacraments be administered in accordance with the divine Word. It is not necessary for the true unity of the Christian church that ceremonies, instituted by men, should be observed uniformly in all places. It is as Paul says in Ephesians 4:4–5, "There is one body and one Spirit, just as you were called to the one hope that belongs to your call, one Lord, one faith, one baptism."

A Reading from the New Testament
[God] has put all things under his feet and has made [Christ] the head over all things for the church, which

is his body, the fullness of him who fills all in all (Ephesians 1:22–23).

Reflection

Our Reformation ancestors were not engaged in a war of independence, breaking away from the Catholic Church, or starting a new denomination. Yet these are all ways in which their reform movement is often described.

Actually, they introduced their reforms with fear and trembling, aware that what they were doing threatened the unity of the church, eager to demonstrate that they had not broken that unity, and did not want to do so. So they said that Christians can differ about whether or not to do the Mass in German or Latin, about whether or not to have monasteries and convents, about whether or not our priests and pastors marry. But if "the Gospel be preached in conformity with a pure understanding of it" and if "the sacraments be administered in accordance with the divine Word," then the unity of the church has not been broken.

Why was that and is that so important? Because the Gospel of Jesus announced the coming of the kingdom of God (Mark 1:14–15). The kingdom of God is God's project for all of humanity. God set out to reconcile all of humanity, and God did this in the death of Jesus on the cross (Ephesians 2:14–16). The church is called to be a witness to that Gospel, that reconciliation. The church is called to anticipate the unity of all of humanity. If the disciples of Jesus are fragmented, broken, fighting, competing, condemning each other, ignoring each other, or barely tolerating each other, then there is not only negative witness—there is reason actually to doubt whether Jesus is Messiah, whether the kingdom of God has come, whether we ought to be Christians at all. That's why giving expression to the unity of the church is so important.

That unity has already been created by God through Christ's offering of himself on the cross. That is the great vision that our Reformation ancestors discovered in the Holy Scriptures. "For he is our peace; in his flesh he has made both groups [Jews and Gentiles] into one and has broken down the dividing wall, that is, the hostility between us. He has abolished the law with its commandments and ordinances, that he might create in himself one new humanity in place of the two, thus making peace, and might reconcile both groups to God in one body through the cross, thus putting to death that hostility through it. So he came and proclaimed peace to you who were far off and peace to those who were near; for through him both of us have access in one Spirit to the Father" (Ephesians 2:14–18). The unity we have been given by the Triune God is the unity we are called to embody in the church (John 17:22–23).

Collect

Your Word and your bread are our life's essentials, O Lord Jesus Christ. Speak to us your Word of grace, and feed us with the Bread of Life, that we may be your church, with body, mind, and spirit properly nourished for your holy work. Amen.

Congregational Prayer

Lord Jesus Christ, as members of your Body, the Church, use us and the gifts you give us as you see fit.

Our expectant hope is to be with you for eternity. You will keep your promises and stand over our graves and wake us up to new life. We foresee the day when the work we've done for you on earth will be transformed into good work, kingdom work, and useful training for the world to come. We anticipate being your disciples forever, in worlds and work unknown to us now, except through imagination.

Fill us with the sanctity of this moment in worship together. You know the true membership of your church. Remind us of the cross, lest our beliefs be haughty or glib. Remind us of the widow's mite when we think we have too little to be of use to you. Remind us of your Holy Meal and your Holy Word, so that our Baptism and redemption will have daily meaning for us.

As we learn to delight in being among your church people, fill us with the joy of knowing that people in every land love you as we do. With them, whose hearts you form and free, let us work and serve and be your holy family. Amen.

Personal Prayer

Lord Jesus Christ, help me love my brother and sister when they aren't very lovable. They are your children, your church, your targets for grace, and without them, I am poorer. Without them I remain a part of their problem, and I become a problem to myself.

In so many ways it is easier to love you, O Lord, than it is to love the people of your church. People are hard on me. I am hard on them too. We do not get along that well ... quick to judge, and slow to forgive. But your Word and your Holy Meal melt me. You feed soul to me ... your soul, your body, your blood, your Word. In you is no hardness at all. And you tell me to be this same way toward those who are not being good to me.

Lord, your words are inspiring, but the doing of them is impossible work. It is hard. I cannot be you. I do not have your strength. I am so afraid of losing my self-respect. I don't want to be wronged anymore.

"There is one body, one Spirit, one hope, one Lord, one faith, one Baptism." You give me no other option. I am to be part of your one church, just like all the others, or no part of you at all.

Lord Jesus, open my heart to see your church in everyone who calls you by name. Open my heart to love anyone who loves you. Amen.

What the Church Is

Again, although the Christian church, properly speaking, is nothing else than the assembly of all believers and saints, yet because in this life many false Christians, hypocrites, and even open sinners remain among the godly, the sacraments are efficacious even if the priests who administer them are wicked men, for as Christ himself indicated, "The Pharisees sit on Moses' seat" (Matthew 23:2).

A Reading from the New Testament

Some proclaim Christ from envy and rivalry, but others from goodwill. These proclaim Christ out of love, knowing that I have been put here for the defense of the gospel; the others proclaim Christ out of selfish ambition, not sincerely but intending to increase my suffering in my imprisonment. What does it matter? Just this, that Christ is proclaimed in every way, whether out of false motives or true; and in that I rejoice (Philippians 1:15–18).

Reflection

One year we had an exercise in a senior theology class at seminary. We asked the students to identify those things that made it most difficult for them to believe the Gospel. We thought we would hear about secularism or science or skeptical criticism or the problem of evil. To our surprise, a significant number of students said that what made it most difficult for them to believe the Gospel was—the church!

It is hardly possible for any of us to be active in the church for very long without beginning to collect stories of people in the church who have disappointed us, perhaps hurt us. Those people often include pastors. Worst of all is the realization that we ourselves have surely at times disappointed, perhaps even hurt, other members of the church.

This article should be a great comfort to us all. Our Reformation ancestors were realists. Martin Luther said, "The church is an inn and a hospital for the sick and those who are being cured." The Triune God is the backing for the promises of the Gospel, not the morality of the members or the integrity of the clergy. God is faithful, even when we are not. God will not let us down, even when human trustworthiness is fragile and broken.

Collect

Lord God of all creation, you use even the acts of sinful people among us to work your will and effect your power. You have divided Satan's house against him, by letting Christ come despite the unbelief of those who often name your Name. Keep us from being among the hypocrites who do not believe, but only use your name for personal benefit. Amen.

Congregational Prayer

Lord Jesus Christ, as your Body, the Church, we are a most soiled lot. None of our washing makes us clean. None of our costly clothing covers who we are. Our smiles do not erase the pain we seek to hide, and if we are blessed enough to be able to walk with confident stride, still we know that we are acting ... living by a power of positive thinking, but not of positive God-given faith.

Come to us, dear Lord, with your Word. Feed us your Holy Meal. Remind us of our Holy Baptism. Speak holy words to us ... words that the world cannot hear nor understand, though the syllables are public, and all the sounds are audible.

When you say "My blood, my body," help us sense our body and blood engulfed by yours. When you say, "I baptize you," help us hear the love in your voice that says "My most precious child."

When you say, "Your sins are forgiven," give us the faith we cannot create on our own; the faith that dares to believe you did it. You forgave it. The sin is gone. Your love is not diminished. We are free to be a person again. We need not, should not, must not doubt it. We will not let the failure keep coming back to haunt us with guilt, or rob us of peace. We will not doubt your power to renew us.

This power is yours alone to give, dear Lord, and you will to give it more than we will to receive it. Replace the faith we've tried to manufacture on our own with the faith you give to children alone: the faith to believe you love us, despite all. Amen.

Personal Prayer

Lord Jesus, help me hear you calling me when you call your people to gather. Whenever you choose to speak, help me want to be a part of your assembly of believers.

Sometimes, Lord, I prefer you all to myself. Sometimes I neglect the places you said you would be—in broken bread, and lifted wine, in the confession of sins among the believers, in the singing of songs with others who sense that this world is not all that there is to your world.

Lord, you give others to me, and you give me to others. You make me rely upon the church for my own soul's sake. You are forever calling me to gather with others. You like to use my sisters and brothers to show me your love. You like to tell me how you got through to them. You like to strengthen me by their witness. You make me relate to you on your own terms.

You just don't want a lonely church, Lord. And you don't want me lonely, either, though sometimes I prefer it. You call me to gather with others. You send me out and give me work to do with others. You make the job too big for me to do alone.

Lord Jesus Christ, it is not good for any one of us to be alone. You call the hypocrite, the saint, the doubter, the unbeliever, and me together. You let us see one another's sinfulness. You don't give up on any one of us. You let us do your work together, but you call us saints by your grace alone. Amen.

ARTICLE 9

Baptism

It is taught among us that Baptism is necessary and that grace is offered through it. Children, too, should be baptized, for in Baptism they are committed to God and become acceptable to him.

On this account the Anabaptists who teach that infant Baptism is not right are rejected.

A Reading from the New Testament

Do you not know that all of us who have been baptized into Christ Jesus were baptized into his death? Therefore we have been buried with him by baptism into death, so that, just as Christ was raised from the dead by the glory of the Father, so we too might walk in newness of life (Romans 6:3–4).

A Reading from the Old Testament

The hand of the Lord came upon me, and he brought me out by the spirit of the Lord and set me down in the middle of a valley; it was full of bones. He led me all around them; there were very many lying in the valley, and they were very dry. He said to me, "Mortal, can these bones live?" I answered, "O Lord God, you know." Then he said to me, "Prophesy to these bones, and say to them: O dry bones, hear the word of the Lord. Thus says the Lord God to these bones: I will cause breath to enter you, and you shall live. I will lay sinews on you, and will cause flesh to come upon you, and cover you with skin, and put breath in you, and you shall live; and you shall know that I am the Lord." ...

Then he said to me, "Mortal, these bones are the whole house of Israel. They say, 'Our bones are dried up, and our hope is lost; we are cut off completely.' Therefore prophesy, and say to them, Thus says the Lord God: I am going to open your graves, and bring you up from your graves, O my people; and I will bring you back to the land of Israel. And you shall know that I am the Lord, when I open your graves, and bring you up from your graves, O my people. I will put my spirit within you, and you shall live, and I will place you on your own soil; then you shall know that I, the Lord, have spoken and will act," says the Lord (Ezekiel 37:1–6, 11–14).

Reflection

Birth and death go together, and that is their normal sequence as well. First we are born, and then we die.

But the God "who gives life to the dead and calls into existence the things that do not exist" (Romans 4:17) has added a new chapter to that sequence. After birth and death comes new birth. The new birth is called "Baptism." In Baptism we are put to death with Christ, and then, with him, we are given new life. The new life is like a change of clothing. "As God's chosen ones, holy and beloved, clothe yourselves with compassion, kindness, humility, meekness, and patience. Bear with one another and, if anyone has a complaint against another, forgive each other; just as the Lord has forgiven you, so you also must forgive. Above all, clothe yourselves with love, which binds everything together in perfect harmony. And let the peace of Christ rule in your hearts, to which indeed you were called in the one body. And be thankful" (Colossians 3:12–15).

Collect

God of grace, by our Baptisms you made us your children. You are our Heavenly Father for all time. As your children, teach us to be joyfully dependent upon you for all good things and to trust you with our well-being. Amen.

Congregational Prayer

Lord God Almighty, without our advice or consent you gave us life through birth and Baptism. Without our consent you adopted us through Baptism, made us your own, and loved us beyond our understanding.

It is in your name, Lord Jesus, that we have been baptized. You, with the Heavenly Father and the Holy Spirit, love us. You make the Baptism joyful, for we are not only baptized like you for this lifetime, but resurrected like you for the life to come.

Holy Spirit, you keep calling us back to our Baptism so that we might gather with the faithful to hear God's word, receive forgiveness, and have the will to seek God's will for our daily life. You do this out of sheer love for us, to keep us from seeking to make our way in life without you.

Father, Son, and Holy Spirit you shower us with gifts beyond our merit or understanding. What you did for us on the day of our Baptism, you do for us this day also. You adopt us today, make us your own today, and love us beyond our understanding today.

Help us accept this pure grace from you without hesitancy. Keep us from adding any condition to your love. Let us trust you like children trust loving parents. Amen.

Personal Prayer

Lord God, I was committed to you through Baptism, without having a word to say about it. Regardless of my age, I was given over to you like an infant child. Ever since, I've been trying to make myself your worthy child.

Sometimes I have decided not to be your child. Sometimes I try to add my own vows and promises to my Baptism, so that I can claim some part in the adoption. You keep smiling at me winsomely, knowing that all of my attempts to make you love me are unnecessary and impossible futile acts.

You deny me any part in making me your child. You simply say "my daughter, my son." You don't wait for me to grow up and love you. You don't wait for me to serve you. You don't walk away from me when I walk away from you. You just won't disappear.

Holy Father, you alone are the example of perfect parenthood. No one of us can attain it. You give, knowing that I have nothing of worth to return to you. You give, knowing that I cannot always be good. You give, knowing that I will not always talk nicely about you.

It is humbling, Lord, to be so dependent upon you for my own salvation, but I know that I have no power to save my own life. It is your work alone.

May my life be a ceaseless thank-you to you, Lord Jesus. May I give and pray and live as you teach, and may I die looking in joy for the resurrection, believing that I have been baptized into your death, as well as into your life. Amen.

ARTICLE 10

The Holy Supper of Our Lord

It is taught among us that the true body and blood of Christ are really present in the Supper of our Lord under the form of bread and wine and are there distributed and received. The contrary doctrine is therefore rejected.

A Reading from the New Testament

When you come together, it is not really to eat the Lord's supper. For when the time comes to eat, each of you goes ahead with your own supper, and one goes hungry and another becomes drunk. What! Do you not have homes to eat and drink in? Or do you show contempt for the church of God and humiliate those who have nothing? What should I say to you? Should I commend you? In this matter I do not commend you!

For I received from the Lord what I also handed on to you, that the Lord Jesus on the night when he was betrayed took a loaf of bread, and when he had given thanks, he broke it and said, "This is my body that is for you. Do this in remembrance of me." In the same way he took the cup also, after supper, saying, "This cup is the new covenant in my blood. Do this, as often as you drink it, in remembrance of me." For as often as you eat this bread and drink the cup, you proclaim the Lord's death until he comes (1 Corinthians 11:20–26).

Reflection

Christians have had many and bitter arguments about whether and how the Lord is present to us and with us in the Christian meal, the Holy Eucharist. The arguments go back at least as far as one of the earliest Christian communities, the church in Corinth, around the year A.D. 50. St. Paul's word is quite clear: Jesus is indeed with us, and he is with us as the one who offers himself into death for us.

But there is more. His presence as the offered one takes place in a community of believers who receive his offering by offering themselves for each other and for the world. St. Paul is also clear about one more thing: If we use Christ's offering of himself as the occasion for not recognizing the needs of others, if we indulge ourselves instead of offering ourselves, then our meal is not the Lord's Supper. Then we might as well stay at home; we are not the church. For the church is the community of people who receive Christ's offering by offering themselves.

Collect

Lord Jesus Christ, help us to discern your presence in this Holy Meal, that we may receive your body and blood as your beloved family. Amen.

Congregational Prayer

Lord Jesus Christ, through your Holy Supper, you make it clear that it is not good to eat alone, so you join yourself to us as host. Your true presence makes the meal a banquet.

Jesus, Lamb of God, your sacrificial body and blood mingle within us, so that we might not ever doubt your presence. You will not be kept at arm's length. You will not be just a distant friend or teacher. You intimately join yourself to us in the breaking of bread and prayers.

Though we are not worthy to be your guests, you keep inviting us back. You invite us to open our hearts to you, even as you open your heart to us.

Your heart tells us of love so deep that no one can repay you. Your heart tells us of power so great that no one needs to fear the future. Your heart tells us of life coming, and a reunion banquet so glorious, that all of death's dirty work is over. You make hope an expectation. You pull back the curtain on the next world, and show us we'll be there with you.

Holy Lord of the divine presence, focus our hearts and minds on you. Make this meal, this worship, this day, and this week holy, for we are your guests. May we hear your invitation, "Come, dear child of mine, and be my guest." Amen.

Personal Prayer

Lord Jesus Christ, I cannot stand for one moment in your presence without your invitation and permission. You are beyond me in reason, beauty, and power. You are more than I can bear, unless you allow me to enter into the joy of your presence.

Your grace, dear Lord, comes as torrent in the Holy Communion. You sweep over me like a flood, as your vein opens up on my behalf. I would be washed away forever, if you did not hold me fast. I cannot bear to see you, unless you shield my eyes.

My dear host, when you protect me from all the ravages of my mind, you speak most softly and eloquently, like one who has all knowledge, no fear, and no guile. You simply remind me that you have been through death, and I will be all right. You remind me that you have an agenda for this world that I cannot fathom. You assure me that the Father is loving, that the Spirit is caring, and that you wish to be my friend, a friend who will never forsake me.

Lord Jesus Christ, throughout the ages you have fed your people with your body and blood. All the company of heaven rejoices when you are near. Now hear my thanks, as one of them. Care for those separated from me by death. And remind me that our separation is only for a little while. Amen.

ARTICLE 11

Confession

It is taught among us that private absolution should be retained and not allowed to fall into disuse. However, in confession it is not necessary to enumerate all trespasses and sins, for this is impossible. Psalm 19:12, "Who can discern his errors?"

Readings from the New Testament

Therefore confess your sins to one another, and pray for one another, so that you may be healed (James 5:16).

My friends, if anyone is detected in a transgression, you who have received the Spirit should restore such a one in a spirit of gentleness. Take care that you yourselves are not tempted. Bear one another's burdens, and in this way you will fulfill the law of Christ (Galatians 6:1–2).

Reflection

The sins of others, when we become aware of them, confront us with three options. We can ignore them. Or we can become accusers, which then gives us a sense of superiority over those whose sins have been detected and exposed. Or we can restore them "in a spirit of gentleness." To forgive is to share the burden of sin. Forgiveness is not overlooking sin. It is overcoming sin. To forgive the sins of those who sin against us is the ultimate in sharing the burden. Instead of seeking to repel the inflicted hurt by an act of "getting even," we overcome the sin by sharing the burden. Because we do not always know when we have sinned against others, we are free in the Gospel to welcome their admonition, to confess our sin, and to receive forgiveness. The sign of forgiveness is so powerful that Martin Luther can write:

"Whatever can be effected by Baptism and the Lord's Supper, which are appointed as outward signs, this sign also can effect to strengthen and gladden our conscience. And it has been especially instituted for us to use and practice every hour, keeping it with us at all times" ("Large Catechism" 1959, 433).

Therefore, Luther writes, "when I urge you to go to confession, I am simply urging you to be a Christian" ("Large Catechism" 1959, 460).

Collect

Hear our confession of sin, Lord, so that we may hear your absolution and work toward amendment of life. Hear our confession of sin, Lord, that we may know our need of you forever. Hear our confession of sin, Lord, and turn our sorrow into joyous forgiveness and renewal. Amen.

Congregational Prayer

Lord Jesus Christ, you have heard our confession of sin, and we ask that we may hear your absolution. We need to hear it out loud, not just within, for the sake of certainty.

We remember your passion, the betrayal, the trial, the walk to Golgotha, the cross, your disciples in hiding, and your mother in deep grief with John the Beloved nearby. We remember the great cost to you for the forgiveness of our sins.

We remember, too, that we have confessed our sins before and will have to do so again. Increase our will to do your will, so that holiness of life may be both a heartfelt thank-you for your forgiveness, and a commitment to follow you more closely.

Speak your forgiving word, Lord, and let us receive it like children receiving mercy from a loving parent. Speak your absolution, and remove all doubt but that our sin is gone forever and need not be recounted again. Give us your mercy, Lord, and help us give mercy to others who need a word of reconciliation from us. Amen.

Personal Prayer

Lord Jesus, I am reluctant to share my sins with any other human being. I do not want others to think less of me than they already do. I do not want word of my wrong-doing to be known. I would keep all of my weakness private, Lord, and put up a good appearance.

Lord, these admissions are admissions of sin. You know how vain I am, how selfish, how weak in faith. You know how I struggle with wanting to be loved and seeking joy through things. You know how I like to avoid conflict and ignore the needs of others. I simply want to stop having to change my ways.

Sometimes, Lord, I feel like I'm a lump of clay on your potter's wheel. I am satisfied with the first shape that appears, but you keep knocking me down and starting me over. Won't you ever be done with me?

Lord, don't ever be done with me. Help me look forward with fascination to the new life you make out of sorry clay like me. Help me see how every past crushing experience has been a gift from you to make me more nearly your own. Help me not fear the change that you bring to those you love.

Hear my confession of sin, Lord, as a confession of faith, that you will love me regardless, forgive me most readily, and show me a more excellent way to live this life as your disciple. Amen.

ARTICLE 12

Repentance

It is taught among us that those who sin after Baptism receive forgiveness of sin whenever they come to repentance, and absolution should not be denied them by the church. Properly speaking, true repentance is nothing else than to have contrition and sorrow, or terror, on account of sin, and yet at the same time to believe the Gospel and absolution (namely, that sin has been forgiven and grace has been obtained through Christ), and this faith will comfort the heart and again set it at rest. Amendment of life and the forsaking of sin should then follow, for these must be the fruits of repentance, as John says, "Bear fruit that befits repentance" (Matthew 3:8).

Rejected here are those who teach that persons who have once become godly cannot fall again.

Condemned on the other hand are the Novatians who denied absolution to such as had sinned after Baptism.

Rejected also are those who teach that forgiveness of sin is not obtained through faith but through the satisfaction made by man.

A Reading from the New Testament

Now after John was arrested, Jesus came to Galilee, proclaiming the good news of God, and saying, "The time is fulfilled, and the kingdom of God has come near; repent, and believe in the good news" (Mark 1:14–15).

Reflection

The Lutheran Reformation began as a crisis in pastoral care. Persons had come to believe that by purchasing a "letter of indulgence" they were free from ever having to go to confession again. Martin Luther preached, "Would that I were a liar when I say that indulgences are rightly so called, for to indulge means to permit, and indulgence is equivalent to impunity, permission to sin, and license to nullify the cross of Christ" (Sermon on Indulgences, 1517). Without repentance we indulge ourselves.

Repentance simply means to see things in a new way. It means, therefore, that we recognize and confess as sin whatever is truly sin. When we repent, we stop justifying ourselves. We are set free by the justifying cross of Christ to see ourselves in truth, to repent, to confess. Without the gift of repentance we will never be free to do battle with our sins.

Collect

Turn us around, Lord God Almighty, from a daily quest for personal happiness to a daily quest to be your people. We repent of our selfishness, which has not brought us joy, and ask you to intervene mightily in our lives, that your will may take precedence over our own. Amen.

Congregational Prayer

Lord God Almighty, we come as a family of faith admitting that we need forgiveness for our sins.

We have not sought out your will for our lives. Some of us have felt little terror or dread over the consequences of our sins. In so doing, we continue to ignore the pain brought to others through our selfishness. Some of us have felt only terror and dread, and have not learned to accept your grace. And some of us have not yet learned to forgive one another, though we accept forgiveness from you for our personal wrongdoing.

Lord, keep us from believing that all there is to repentance is admission of wrongdoing. Through true repentance, help us amend our lives, forsake selfishness, accept your forgiveness, and forgive one another.

Christ, show us the way again. Let us not be terrified of the cross. Let us not be afraid to forgive, or to be forgiven. Let goodness and mercy follow us all the days of our lives. Let the promise of dwelling with you forever be our constant hope. Amen.

Personal Prayer

Lord Jesus Christ, forgiver of my sin, how am I to believe that you really do take away my sin, as well as the sin of the whole world? I still feel rotten after sinning. I still feel rotten after repenting. I am not able to let go of my sense of worthlessness to you and to the world. I repent, hear your forgiving word, and repent again of the same misdeed. I cannot stop sinning.

If true repentance is not only admission of wrong, but a changing of life, please help me change. I am weary of myself. I long to stop doubting your work on my behalf. What repentance do you want out of me? What am I neglecting to note? Where is my wrong heart beneath my wrong deed?

Lord Jesus, if you answer my several questions, and I am stricken with a terror of myself beyond mere disappointment, be there to pick me up and start me over again as your new person.

As your new person, Lord, I imagine I would be quite different from what I know myself to be today. I imagine I would follow you more nearly. I imagine I would endure the wrongs of others upon me more patiently. I imagine I would be about doing good works for your sake, and not my own. I imagine I would be totally converted.

Lord Jesus Christ, convert me. By my own power I cannot be what you would have me be. Convert me. Change my heart by entering my heart. Make every day your day. Save me from myself. When my next opportunity for sin approaches, come into my mind and heart immediately.

May peace and joy result not only from this, my repentance, but also from the next time I resist sin, through your power. Amen.

ARTICLE 13

The Use of the Sacraments

It is taught among us that the sacraments were instituted not only to be signs by which people might be identified outwardly as Christians, but that they are signs and testimonies of God's will toward us for the purpose of awakening and strengthening our faith. For this reason they require faith, and they are rightly used when they are received in faith for the purpose of strengthening faith.

A Reading from the New Testament
So those who welcomed [Peter's] message were baptized, and that day about three thousand persons were added. They devoted themselves to the apostles' teaching and fellowship, to the breaking of bread and the prayers (Acts 2:41–42).

Reflection

The sacraments are not only outward signs, but they are at least that. I was riding on a train in Communist-ruled East Germany on a Saturday in 1985 (four years before the reunification of Germany). A mother was explaining to me that her daughter had been selected for the East German swimming program, and if the girl worked hard and did well, there would be many privileges. She might be selected for a future Olympics team, and they might even get to travel abroad. When she asked what I did, I told her that I was a theologian. She was a bit embarrassed as she confessed they were not "churchly." "My daughter is not baptized," she went on. "There are no advantages to being baptized."

The next day, in Eisenach, I was present as a congregation celebrated the Holy Eucharist. In the service, a young couple brought their infant daughter to be baptized. The congregation applauded. They all knew that this was a sign. And there were no privileges attached to Baptism in a Socialist state. But in the signs of Baptism, and the Holy Eucharist, and forgiveness, there are privileges of which those without faith cannot be aware. We are let in on the Gospel, that Christ is risen, and that he has the last word, a word which is "above all rule and authority and power and dominion" (Ephesians 1:21).

Collect

By your command, Lord Jesus Christ, we are baptized and participate in your Holy Supper. Marked as your person through these gifts, our resolve is increased to be your person as our hearts are moved to believe. Amen.

Congregational Prayer

Lord Jesus Christ, we see you in the sacraments of Baptism and Holy Communion most clearly. Your Word is visible in the water, the wine, and the bread. You have commanded us to use your gifts for our own strengthening of faith and to be marked as your person in the world today.

Help us, Lord Jesus, to proudly bear the mark of the cross, both in the worship service of our congregation, and throughout the week. Let every bath remind us of our Baptism, every meal of the banquet that is coming.

As your cross-marked people, may we bear your yoke patiently, knowing that you share the yoke with us. You are bound to us by the crossbeam of the cross. You show that the way of suffering is not to be avoided at all cost. You know what is on the other side of our labors and losses.

The great evil powers of the world are nothing compared to your love. Though Satan rage against us, we have nothing to fear. You will win, and your kingdom has already begun.

As we bear our separate burdens, fill us with courage to be your people. You adopted us in Baptism. You feed us in Holy Communion, and you will resurrect us on the last day. Amen.

Personal Prayer

Bearing your cross, Lord Jesus, is better than bearing

my own. I make my own cross out to be heavier than it really is. I try to carry it all alone. I make my cross out to be a barrier to faith, while all the time you are using it to drive me to you. I make my cross out to be wrong and unnecessary, but you use tools that the world cannot understand.

Lord, you know I have only a toehold in your kingdom because I am so much in love with this world. You know I am drawn to you, but have resisted you too. You know I am all the poorer for my low threshold for injustice against myself, while not noting the greater injustices others bear.

I give thanks for your saints who rejoiced that they were seen fit to bear suffering for your sake. I give thanks for those few moments when you've given me the strength to be your person in adversity. I give thanks for being marked as your person at every Holy Communion service.

Be now, I pray, the great mover of my life. Shift my allegiance, my heart, and my feet from this world to your world. Amen.

ARTICLE 14

Order in the Church

It is taught among us that nobody should publicly teach or preach or administer the sacraments in the church without a regular call.

A Reading from the New Testament

The gifts [Christ] gave were that some would be apostles, some prophets, some evangelists, some pastors and teachers, to equip the saints for the work of ministry, for building up the body of Christ, until all of us come to the unity of the faith and of the knowledge of the Son of God, to maturity, to the measure of the full stature of Christ (Ephesians 4:11–13).

Reflection

In the Augsburg Confession, Article 5 is about the Holy Spirit, although it was later given the title, "The Office of the Ministry." Article 14 is about the ordained pastoral ministry of the church. The church has an ordained pastoral ministry not so that some persons may have a more important place and task in the church, but so that the Word of God and the administration of the sacraments may be served. Some persons are called and set apart by ordination for service to the Gospel. They are charged by the rest of us in the church to be concerned about the authenticity of the Gospel in our midst.

The temptation that all of us face and to which we often succumb is to substitute something for the Gospel, perhaps something that makes us feel good at the expense of others, or something that caters to our prejudices, or something that blesses enterprises and projects that ought not be blessed. So we call and ordain some persons to tend the Gospel, to preach with the power that sets us free to name our sins, to administer sacraments that mark us as Christ's community of hope in the world.

The sinner in us doesn't always want to hear the Gospel, doesn't always want to be marked by the sacraments, doesn't always want to be Christ's community of hope. All the more reason why we sinners need an ordained pastoral ministry, and why we need to sustain that ordained ministry with our prayers. To want authenticity for our own ministries means that we want our ordained ministers to do their appointed work faithfully.

Collect

Lord Jesus, we give thanks that you are present

wherever the Word is rightly taught, and the sacraments rightly administered. Continue to be with us as we seek to be faithful to you. Amen.

Congregational Prayer

As you called the prophets and priests of old, we give you thanks for calling clergy and laity to serve your church. Together we are called upon to do your ministry, not our own. It is your light alone that is reflected when we do your work. Give us your mighty presence that we may not grow weary with one another or in well-doing.

We thank you too, for calling all of us to our daily work. We are witnesses for you in the decisions we make, the words we speak, the burdens we bear, and the people with whom we associate. Give us a sense of your presence and purpose in our everyday lives.

Because we belong to you, Lord Jesus, we dare not think that it is what we do that makes you love us. Give to those who have been hindered from employment, or who serve through suffering or disease, a confidence that you are accomplishing your will through them, often in greater measure than anyone can fathom.

Give to pastors and people a relationship of trust and respect, that your Word may be rightly taught and your sacraments received with joy. Amen.

Personal Prayer

Lord Jesus, your call to follow precedes and dominates your call to lead. Too often I get it backwards. I am ready to jump out in front and be bold. I am ready to make cause for you. I am sure of my motives, and can even anticipate your approval and the applause of the world.

Lord Jesus, thank you for your patience with me. Like St. Peter, you have to keep saying over and over to me: "Follow, follow, follow."

When the water touched my body and I was baptized, you marked me with your cross. When you feed me your body and blood, you remind me it is "body and blood," not mere bread and wine. When I strain at the bit to lead instead of follow, pull in the reins until I know it is your will, not mine, that is guiding the decision.

Give me an ear to hear your call, a will to do your will, and a spirit of humbleness ready to lose the battle gracefully. If that occurs, bind me up, and set me back on course, that I may never cease listening for your Word. Amen.

ARTICLE 15

Church Usages

With regard to church usages that have been established by men, it is taught among us that those usages are to be observed which may be observed without sin and which contribute to peace and good order in the church, among them being certain holy days, festivals, and the like. Yet we accompany these observances with instruction so that consciences may not be burdened by the notion that such things are necessary for salvation.

A Reading from the New Testament

The brothers, both the apostles and the elders, to the believers of Gentile origin in Antioch and Syria and Cilicia, greetings. Since we have heard that certain persons who have gone out from us, though with no instructions from us, have said things to disturb you and have unsettled your minds, we have decided unanimously to choose representatives and send them to you, along with our beloved Barnabas and Paul, who have risked their lives for the sake of our Lord Jesus Christ.... For it has seemed good to the Holy Spirit and to us to impose on you no further burden than these essentials: that you abstain from what has been sacrificed to idols and from blood and from what is strangled and from fornication. If you keep yourselves from these, you will do well (Acts 15:23–29).

Reflection

Christianity began as a messianic movement within Israel. But it became evident to Jesus' earliest disciples that if Jesus is truly the Messiah, then all nations and peoples were to be called to faith and obedience. That is the vision for all of humanity that God has revealed to Israel. The great question for this messianic movement was whether Gentiles, called and baptized into Jesus, the Messiah, were required to obey Torah. Most especially, were they required to be circumcised? The response of the leading Jews in Jerusalem who believed Jesus is the Messiah has served the church well throughout the centuries.

Much as these Jews loved Torah and obeyed it themselves (e.g., Philippians 3:5–6), they knew that Torah was not and could not be constitutive for the community that reconciled Jews and Gentiles in a single humanity (Ephesians 2:15–16). So, in love, they agreed that, although Gentiles did not have to obey Torah at all, and Jews would continue to observe

Torah, all of them, Gentiles and Jews, would observe some of Torah together.

Our Reformation ancestors agreed that we ought to observe whatever "may be observed without sin" and contributes "to peace and good order in the church." So we have agreed to do certain things that are neither commanded nor forbidden in the New Testament. We Lutherans have our children confirmed, use a liturgical order for worship and the celebration of the Holy Communion, and obey the constitution and by-laws of our church. We are not required to do these things as "necessary for salvation." But we voluntarily require them of ourselves for the sake of "peace and good order."

Collect

Accept our worship, God of all creation, as an act of our love for the sending of your Son, Jesus Christ. Keep us from supposing that our songs, prayers, and traditions merit your grace. For what you are alone, we give you our praise. Amen.

Congregational Prayer

We give you thanks for liturgy, good order, and good traditions that remind us of your work among your people in all times. You are the God of ages past, and our hope for years to come. You are the God and Father of us all.

As we listen to your Word, create faith in us through the working of your Holy Spirit. Give us an open heart so that the words of Scripture and sermon, and the taste of bread and wine, will help us discern your presence already among us. You are here in our midst even without our acknowledgment, but we thank you for the visible gifts of bread and wine in the sacrament of Holy Communion, that we might better perceive the reality of your nearness.

Lord Jesus, you are always with us, even when we are far from worshiping you with others. When we are absent, we hear your gathering call through the Holy Spirit, urging us to remember that where two or three are gathered together in your name, you are right there in the middle of things. Help us see you in another's faith. Help us hear you in another's song. Help us taste you in offered bread and wine, as your true body and blood. Open us to your presence, in all of its power, whether it is in a still small voice, a loud clashing cymbal, or the humble faith of another believer at prayer. Amen.

Personal Prayer

Lord Jesus Christ, you are my mediator. Sometimes I try to have you all to myself, without the presence of other Christians. But you keep calling me back to the congregation where you work your wonders among all the faithful, not just me. You keep calling me to discover the words of the faithful departed, whom you called and chose to be your voice and presence in their time.

Through printed word you have opened to me the prayers and musings of your saints and my forebears. Keep me from neglecting their discoveries. Help me learn from them by honoring your work through their words and wisdom. Especially, dear Lord, keep me from copying their outward example, without living the faith.

Through my daily work, create in me such a sense of your presence, that even menial tasks become gifts to you for the sake of your kingdom. Hallow my work, my time, and my life, that I may worship you by deed as well as by word. Amen.

ARTICLE 16

Civil Government

It is taught among us that all government in the world and all established rule and laws were instituted and ordained by God for the sake of good order, and that Christians may without sin occupy civil offices or serve as princes and judges, render decisions and pass sentence according to imperial and other existing laws, punish evildoers with the sword, engage in just wars, serve as soldiers, buy and sell, take required oaths, possess property, be married, etc....

Also condemned are those who teach that Christian perfection requires the forsaking of house and home, wife and child, and the renunciation of such activities as are mentioned above. Actually, true perfection consists alone of proper fear of God and real faith in God.... Christians are obliged to be subject to civil authority and obey its commands and laws in all that can be done without sin. But when commands of the civil authority cannot be obeyed without sin, we must obey God rather than men (Acts 5:29).

A Reading from the New Testament

So they watched [Jesus] and sent spies who pretended to be honest, in order to trap him by what he said, so as to hand him over to the jurisdiction and authority of the governor. So they asked him, "Teacher, we know that you are right in what you say and teach, and you show deference to no one, but teach the way of God in accordance with truth. Is it lawful for us to pay taxes to the emperor, or not?" But he perceived their craftiness and said to them, "Show me a denarius. Whose head and whose title does it bear?" They said, "The emperor's." He said to them, "Then give to the emperor the things that are the emperor's, and to God the things that are God's." And they were not able in the presence of the people to trap him by what he said; and being amazed by his answer, they became silent (Luke 20:20–26).

Reflection

Life in civil community gives us order, opportunity for life, institutions for service, peace, and justice. The Augsburg Confession commits us to receiving the blessing of the civil community with thanksgiving and to participating in its institutions willingly, with a very important qualification: that we do so without sin! Our Reformation ancestors teach us quite clearly that the authority of civil government is always relative. Only God has an absolute claim upon us.

The problem for each of us is how this works out in practice. According to this article, for example, we cannot participate in all wars, only in just wars. That means *selective* conscientious participation in national wars. Just at this point we Lutherans (and members of most Christian traditions) are in conflict with national law. For national law permits either unconditional conscientious objection to war (in which case we are allowed to do alternative service) or unconditional obedience to our government's war policy.

So we muddle through this and hope that we never have to decide about the justice of a war. But if we did have to decide, would we know how? What constitutes a just war? When is a war unjust? The conflict in Vietnam forced these questions upon us, and for the most part we were woefully unprepared to deal with them.

The Augsburg Confession requires us to deal with them. And it requires us to deal with welfare policies, tax policies, educational policies, environmental policies, weapons policies, and many other things that require us to ask: Can we do this without sin? In a democracy we are involved in making policy as well as being obedient to policy. Do we think carefully and clearly about what the policies ought to be? How can we decide? The churches of the Augsburg Confession ought to be communities of lively learning, discussion, and debate about these important questions and policies.

Collect

Continue your work, O Lord, through the political governments of the nations. Provide sustenance for the poor, a voice to the powerless, redress for the wronged, that together we may live with one another in peace and harmony as one respected family on earth. Amen.

Congregational Prayer

God of the nations, bring your Spirit of dignity and worth to every human being in every stage of life. Help us see the face of Christ wherever suffering or need occurs. As your beloved children, may our brothers and sisters in every place be dear to us. Help us see each other as your child, and every child as our child.

We ask that you would counsel the judges and rulers of the lands, that their decisions will be made from conscience and conviction formed by you. We ask you to protect those who are called to the duty of enforcing just laws, both at home and abroad, through armed forces or police squads. Be with those who serve the injured, the sick, the lonely, and the depressed.

Keep us from letting these petitions be our only response to our sisters and brothers in need.

Keep us bound one to another, that no life, however fragile, is dispensed with unnecessarily. You have bound us together. May we always be bound to you. Amen.

Personal Prayer

Lord Jesus Christ, you took the time to heal Peter's mother-in-law, to provide wine at a marriage feast for a bride and groom, to raise sons and daughters from the dead in order to restore families. You fed the whole multitude, and at the end of your earthly life, you provided for your mother by making her and John a family.

Help me support hospitals, nursing homes, orphanages, and homes for mercy, institutions you bless with your miraculous powers. Help me understand that you use people like me to work your miracles today.

Lord Jesus, you use the gifts of heathens to work your will. I wish to be of use to you too.

Lord Jesus, you use the decisions of despots without their will, to bring about relief to the downtrodden. Use me too.

Give to me the gift of stewardship. Help me want this gift, as Bach wanted to make music for you. May I see you trusting me in all of the possessions I call my own. As I use those things you've given to me in trust, help me remember your examples of love. Amen.

The Return of Christ to Judgment

It is also taught among us that our Lord Jesus Christ will return on the last day for judgment and will raise up all the dead, to give eternal life and everlasting joy to believers and the elect but to condemn ungodly men and the devil to hell and eternal punishment.

Readings from the New Testament

Do not fear those who kill the body but cannot kill the soul; rather fear him who can destroy both soul and body in hell (Matthew 10:28).

For as all die in Adam, so all will be made alive in Christ (1 Corinthians 15:22).

Reflection

Karl Barth, a great theologian of the twentieth century, once said that a Christian would have to be crazy to teach universal salvation, but impious not to believe it. For to believe the Gospel is to believe that God's final judgment is life, not death, grace, not eternal condemnation. Many theologians are now saying that, in its history, Christianity has more often threatened the outcast with the fire of damnation than announced to them God's unconditional salvation.

This article of the Augsburg Confession commits us to confess that our Lord Jesus Christ will return to "condemn ungodly men and the devil to hell and eternal punishment." This is a difficult article for us to confess. In our struggle with the paradox of the judgment and the mercy of God, it helps to remember Martin Luther's teaching that both the Law and the Gospel are the Word of God, but we are called to believe the Gospel against the Law. It may be that we are called to trust God's Word of unconditional salvation against God's Word that some human beings will be condemned "to hell and eternal punishment."

The great good news of Christianity is that in the resurrection of Jesus from the dead, the Triune God has revealed the identity of the final judge. Jesus is the Messiah, the final judge of the living and the dead. St. Paul states his unshakable faith in God's mercy in many places. Ponder two of them: "The Son of God, Jesus Christ, whom we proclaimed among you, Silvanus and Timothy and I, was not 'Yes and No'; but in him it is always 'Yes.' For in him every one of God's promises is a 'Yes.' For this reason it is through him that we say the 'Amen,' to the glory of God" (2 Corinthians 1:19–20). "God has imprisoned all in disobedience so that he may be merciful to all" (Romans 11:32).

Collect

Come, Lord Jesus come, when the time is right, and usher in your kingdom in all its fullness. Come, Lord Jesus, come right now as we gather in your name to be your people of faith. Amen.

Congregational Prayer

Heavenly Father, your day of judgment is coming like a thief in the night, and all the world will be surprised.

Heavenly Father, your purposes for this earth and our lives are deeper than our minds can fathom. You have been in combat with our enemy, Satan. Earth and our hearts have become the battleground. You sent your beloved Son, Jesus, to show us how to overcome our enemy, and you are sending him back to consummate his victory.

If it were not for Jesus, dear God, we would face the coming day of judgment with pure dread. No one of us can stand before your throne without him at our side. No one of us can find adequate excuse for our behavior. We are all condemned already, except for the saving work of Christ.

Come, Lord Jesus, come. Come with your mercy and understanding. Come and end the war between the heavenly hosts and Satan. Come and declare victory. Come and put an end to Satan, death, and sin. Come and take us to our heavenly home, which you have prepared for us. Amen.

Personal Prayer

Lord Jesus Christ, the day of resurrection for all of humankind is also my day of resurrection and judgment.

I like to think that I will be swept up with all the believers and not have to stand alone before the throne. I like to think that all the nasty little things I never got rid of will be overlooked with a wink and a smile, and a "That's okay, enter into the joy of your master."

It's more serious than this, isn't it? My wrongdoing and faithlessness required a death, your death, and what I wish to minimize, you paid for by dying.

How can I bear to see your wounds on that day and know that I was among the crowd that chanted "Crucify him?" How can I face you with my record? If you play back my life in all of its sordid detail, I will only be able to weep.

Judgment is humbling, Lord Jesus, and that is a trait I've been loathe to accept as noble. I've wanted to be good enough for your heaven, but you won't let it come that way. I've wanted to help you out with my salvation, but you have said, "No, this is totally my work." I've wanted to please you with my life, and you've said, "Then accept the fact you have been died for, despite yourself."

So this is the final judgment.

Lord Jesus, I come before you as a grateful beggar, forever indebted, and forever glad that you died for me. Amen.

ARTICLE 18

Freedom of the Will

It is also taught among us that man possesses some measure of freedom of the will which enables him to live an outwardly honorable life and to make choices among the things that reason comprehends. But without the grace, help, and activity of the Holy Spirit man is not capable of making himself acceptable to God, of fearing God and believing in God with his whole heart, or of expelling inborn evil lust from his heart. This is accomplished by the Holy Spirit, who is given through the Word of God, for Paul says in 1 Corinthians 2:14, "Natural man does not receive the gifts of the Spirit of God."

A Reading from the New Testament

For we know that the law is spiritual; but I am of the flesh, sold into slavery under sin. I do not understand my own actions. For I do not do what I want, but I do the very thing I hate.... For I know that nothing good dwells within me, that is, in my flesh. I can will what is right, but I cannot do it. For I do not do the good I want, but the evil I do not want is what I do.... Wretched man that I am! Who will rescue me from this body of death? Thanks be to God through Jesus Christ our Lord! (Romans 7:14–25).

Reflection

This article is a brief summary, without the argumentation, of course, of the book Martin Luther thought was his best: *The Bondage of the Will*. We confess regularly that "we are in bondage to sin and cannot free ourselves." Dietrich Bonhoeffer wrote from his prison cell one Advent that we are all like prisoners. The cell door can only be opened from the outside.

The purpose of this article is to glorify the God of the Gospel who breaks through to the world in Jesus Christ, who opens the door of our bondage from the outside.

Collect

Holy Spirit, purify our wills by helping us surrender to the greater will of God. Intervene in our lives, expel Satan, and fill us with the way of Christ, who taught us to pray, "Thy will be done." Amen.

Congregational Prayer

Lord Jesus Christ, the power of our own wills for both good and for evil is frightening. We take pride in our love of life, work, family, and accomplishment. But, we fear our love of self, evil, revenge, and our ability to contemplate even more evil.

Our wills, Lord Jesus, are corrupt. We are in bondage to ourselves. We love ourselves too much. We ask that you would free us by sending the Holy Spirit into us to change our wills forever.

Lord Jesus, you know we need outside help to intervene into our innermost heart of hearts. We need to be cracked open. You know we need a new Spirit to give us a vision of life beyond our own lives. We need your Spirit, your will, even as you sought to do the Heavenly Father's will.

Send your Holy Spirit into our lives that we may truly want God's will to prevail over our own. Send your Holy Spirit into our lives that we may be freed from the horrible need to have everything in life suit us. Send your Holy Spirit into our lives that we may find freedom in yielding to your greater purpose and wisdom. Amen.

Personal Prayer
Lord Jesus, the last thing I shall give you is my will. You know this already.

Lord Jesus, what you want from me, above all else, is my will. I know this already.

How can I give up my will to you, Lord Jesus, and still be me? How can I relinquish what I've come to view as the core of my being, and still be an individual? What about my self-esteem?

My questions reveal my sinfulness so clearly when spoken aloud.

You ask me, "Why would you want to be what you call 'yourself,' for you are miserable as you are?"

You ask me, "How do you know you won't be even more an individual, if you relinquish your core?"

You dare make me question the value of self-esteem. You ask, "Wouldn't you really rather have God's esteem?"

The problem, Lord Jesus, is that there just isn't any way to try it out for a little while. There's no turning back once you crack me open. Then I am vulnerable. I am in your hands, like meat from a pecan nut. Then you have me completely, or I'm just fooling around with you, hardening my shell.

Send your Holy Spirit to me, nut cracker in hand. Now. Do it, Lord Jesus, and don't let me ever look back at these struggles as anything but foolishness on my part.

Come, Holy Spirit. Come. Amen.

ARTICLE 19

The Cause of Sin

It is taught among us that although almighty God has created and still preserves nature, yet sin is caused in all wicked men and despisers of God by the perverted will. This is the will of the devil and of all ungodly men; as soon as God withdraws his support, the will turns away from God to evil. It is as Christ says in John 8:44, "When the devil lies, he speaks according to his own nature."

A Reading from the New Testament

As [Jesus] walked along, he saw a man blind from birth. His disciples asked him, "Rabbi, who sinned, this man or his parents, that he was born blind?" Jesus answered, "Neither this man nor his parents sinned; he was born blind so that God's works might be revealed in him. We must work the works of him who sent me while it is day; night is coming when no one can work. As long as I am in the world, I am the light of the world" (John 9:1–5).

Reflection

This article, in its very brief formulation, takes up the problem of evil in the world. How can Christians confess that God is both creator and preserver of the world and yet not hold God responsible for evil in the world? How can we reconcile the reality of evil on the one hand and the Christian belief in the goodness and power of God on the other hand? There is, finally, no logical answer to this problem; but there is a theological response in the Christian Gospel. I quote two wise theologians who have stated that response eloquently:

"Evil and suffering exist because freedom exists; but freedom has no origin; it is the ultimate frontier. But because freedom exists, God Himself suffers and is crucified. The Divine Love and sacrifice are God's answer to the mystery of freedom wherein evil and suffering have their origin. Divine Love and sacrifice are likewise freedom" (Berdiaev 98).

"God is not in heaven; he is hanging on the cross. Love is not an otherworldly, intruding, self-asserting power and to meditate on the cross can mean to take leave of that dream.... No heaven can rectify Auschwitz. But God, who is not a greater Pharaoh, has justified himself: in sharing the suffering, in sharing the death on the cross" (Soelle 148, 149).

Collect

Cast out our perverted wills, dear God, and cast out our will to sin. Enter into our lives so completely, that our wills are set to obey your commandments and to be your people. Amen.

Congregational Prayer

Creator and preserver of all life, through Jesus your dear Son, you have promised not to withdraw your support from us, even for a moment. You have promised to be with us always, even to the close of the age.

Continue to send your Holy Spirit into our lives. Destroy the power of the evil one within us. Silence the voice that tempts us to neglect the power of your word and the need for your intimate presence.

We ask that you would give us the will to keep our baptismal promises, to reject sin and the power of the devil. We cannot stand up against these forces alone. We ask for your help, for his evil ways are beguiling and his gifts seem so innocent.

If we begin to turn away from you without noticing our own change in direction, call us back loudly and quickly, before it is too late for us to undo the wrong that will certainly occur. Be with us every hour as God and Savior, protector and preserver, for we ask it in the name of him whom you sent, Jesus Christ our Lord. Amen.

Personal Prayer

Lord Jesus, according to the Gospel of John, "When the devil lies, he speaks according to his own nature."

When I lie, sometimes even when I pray, I reflect that same evil nature.

Sometimes I ask you for help, Lord Jesus, with no intention of taking it, or making so much as a single change for you.

I promise devotion, but find myself wrapped up in my own little world as soon as the words exit my mouth.

I conjure up great deeds and valor on your behalf, but wilt at the moment of truth.

I even say "I love you," meaning that I want you to love me, care for me, approve of me, give me your grace, with nary a gift from me.

How I love cheap grace! How fearful I am of obedience to your way!

I let "theology" keep me from obedience, fearing "works righteousness." I lie back passively and let you save me. I forget you talked about a new life, not just new thoughts about God. You, like the psalmists, stopped talking about God to others, and talked with God yourself. You became obedient, even unto death.

My belief comes hard because I do not want the burden of obedience. Dear Lord, help me believe, that I may obey. Help me obey, that I may believe, even unto death. Amen.

ARTICLE 20

Faith and Good Works

Our teachers have been falsely accused of forbidding good works....

We begin by teaching that our works cannot reconcile us with God or obtain grace for us, for this happens only through faith, that is, when we believe that our sins are forgiven for Christ's sake, who alone is the mediator who reconciles the Father. Whoever imagines that he can accomplish this by works, or that he can merit grace, despises Christ and seeks his own way to God, contrary to the Gospel.

This teaching about faith is plainly and clearly treated by Paul in many passages, especially in Ephesians 2:8–9, "For by grace you have been saved through faith; and this is not your own doing, it is the gift of God—not because of works, lest any man should boast."

Although this teaching is held in great contempt among untried people, yet it is a matter of experience that weak and terrified consciences find it most comforting and salutary. The conscience cannot come to rest and peace through works, but only through faith, that is, when it is assured and knows that for Christ's sake it has a gracious God, as Paul says in Romans 5:1, "Since we are justified by faith, we have peace with God."

It is also taught among us that good works should and must be done, not that we are to rely on them to earn grace but that we may do God's will and glorify him. It is always faith alone that apprehends grace and forgiveness of sin. When through faith the Holy Spirit is given, the heart is moved to do good works.

A Reading from the New Testament

But be doers of the word, and not merely hearers who deceive themselves. For if any are hearers of the word and not doers, they are like those who look at themselves in a mirror; for they look at themselves and, on going away, immediately forget what they were like. But those who look into the perfect law, the law of liberty, and persevere, being not hearers who forget but doers who act—they will be blessed in their doing.

If any think they are religious, and do not bridle their tongues but deceive their hearts, their religion is worthless. Religion that is pure and undefiled before God, the Father, is this: to care for orphans and widows in their distress, and to keep oneself unstained by the world (James 1:22–27).

Reflection

We come back again to one of the great theological and ethical problems that has afflicted Lutheran Christians. If we are justified by faith alone, are works excluded, as St. Paul seems to imply (Romans 3:27)? Our Reformation ancestors made a careful distinction. They knew, as we know, that St. Paul ardently exhorted us to do good works, as we can see from the letters to the Corinthians, Romans 12 to 16, Galatians 5 and 6. They also knew that St. Paul equally ardently proclaimed God's grace and exhorted us to trust that grace alone. Now comes the distinction, as quoted above:

"It is also taught among us that good works should and must be done, not that we are to rely on them to earn grace but that we may do God's will and glorify him. It is always faith alone that apprehends grace and forgiveness of sin. When through faith the Holy Spirit is given, the heart is moved to do good works."

It has often been said that we ought to believe as if everything depended upon God, and we ought to live as if everything depended on us. I think that is wrong. If we listen carefully to the distinctions made in this article we might better say: Believe as if everything depended upon God, for it does. Live as if everything depended upon God, for it does. Then you will be free to offer yourselves in love, to give God the obedience that comes only from faith.

Collect

Pardon us, Lord God Almighty, from all our sins, and

through gratitude to you for forgiveness, give us the will to do good works. Amen.

Congregational Prayer
Gracious God, because of your Son Jesus Christ, you have forgiven us our sins. We are at peace with you.

We ask you to let us be of use to you, now that we have been reconciled through Christ. We ask that you would guide us in doing good works. We want to say "thank you" for Jesus' love and for sending him to us.

Guide us as a congregation as we seek to be about your business of caring for those in need. We especially ask you to give us the courage of our convictions, and to reach out with patience and gentleness to those who have yet to come to know your way, feel your mercy, or sing your praise.

Lord Jesus, you have freed us from the fear of death and bondage to sin. You have freed us up for good works. By our good works, know that we are grateful. By our good works, may our faith find expression.

God of all goodness, let good flow from us like it does from you. Help us return good for evil, joy for scorn, love for hate, peace for turmoil. Help us turn the other cheek and deny ourselves all revenge. Use us as examples of Christ in the world. Amen.

Personal Prayer
Lord Jesus, help me persevere in the faith and not lose the gift of doing good works for others.

Because of your grace, I look at my sisters and brothers differently. They no longer look so foreign.

Those who believe look like they have received something from you. Those who don't believe look like they need something from you.

Lord, I have been reluctant to do good works for many reasons. I don't want my gift rejected. I don't want it taken for granted. I don't want to expose more of my heart than I can bear to let another person see. I don't want to be laughed at. I don't want to be thought of as simply "nice."

How Satan still works to thwart good works! How he manipulates me! He is out to undo the freedom you give through salvation. He is out to make good works look like weak work, an enemy to good theology.

All the world, Lord Jesus, is waiting for an honest giver. You are the one.

All the world would like a free lunch. You give grace instead.

All the world would like to know that somewhere, someone loves without any need for something in return. Help them find you.

All the world wishes that goodness could be good, and not tainted with strings and attachments. Help them know the joy of your salvation.

Lord Jesus, in giving me your unconditional love, you make it possible for me to do likewise. Open my heart to the moment of opportunity, and give my will the courage to do it. Amen.

ARTICLE 21

The Cult of Saints

It is also taught among us that saints should be kept in remembrance so that our faith may be strengthened when we see what grace they received and how they were sustained by faith. Moreover, their good works are to be an example for us, each of us in his own calling....

However, it cannot be proved from the Scriptures that we are to invoke saints or seek help from them. "For there is one mediator between God and men, Christ Jesus" (1 Timothy 2:5), who is the only saviour, the only highpriest, advocate, and intercessor before God (Romans 8:34). He alone has promised to hear our prayers. Moreover, according to the Scriptures, the highest form of divine service is sincerely to seek and call upon this same Jesus Christ in every time of need. "If anyone sins, we have an advocate with the Father, Jesus Christ the righteous" (1 John 2:1).

Readings from the New Testament

Therefore, since we are surrounded by so great a cloud of witnesses, let us also lay aside every weight and the sin that clings so closely, and let us run with perseverance the race that is set before us, looking to Jesus the pioneer and perfecter of our faith, who for the sake of the joy that was set before him endured the cross, disregarding its shame, and has taken his seat at the right hand of the throne of God (Hebrews 12:1–2).

After this I looked, and there was a great multitude that no one could count, from every nation, from all tribes and peoples and languages, standing before the throne and before the Lamb, robed in white, with palm branches in their hands. They cried out in a loud voice, saying,

"Salvation belongs to our God who is seated on the throne, and to the Lamb!"

And all the angels stood around the throne and around the elders and the four living creatures, and they fell on their faces before the throne and worshiped God, singing,

"Amen! Blessing and glory and wisdom and thanksgiving and honor and power and might be to our God forever and ever! Amen."

Then one of the elders addressed me, saying, "Who are these, robed in white, and where have they come from?" I said to him, "Sir, you are the one that knows." Then he said to me,

"These are they who have come out of the great ordeal; they have washed their robes and made them white in the blood of the Lamb. For this reason they are before the throne of God, and worship him day and night within his temple, and the one who is seated on the throne will shelter them. They will hunger no more, and thirst no more; the sun will not strike them, nor any scorching heat; for the Lamb at the center of the throne will be their shepherd, and he will guide them to springs of the water of life, and God will wipe away every tear from their eyes" (Revelation 7:9–17).

Reflection

Our Reformation ancestors were quite clear in this article. The saints of the church are to be remembered, not worshiped. They are to be held before us as examples of faith, hope, and love. How should we do this?

One way is to name our congregations after the saints. We Lutherans have tended to limit the saints after whom we have named our congregations to saints mentioned in the New Testament. There are a few Lutheran congregations named after St. Lawrence (Roman deacon and martyr in A.D. 258), St. Martin of Tours (who died in A.D. 397), St. Elizabeth of Thuringia (who died in A.D. 1231), and St. Catherine of Siena (who died in A.D. 1380). Mostly, Lutherans have ignored the "cloud of witnesses" who have been the church's examples throughout the past 1800 years.

A second way is to observe the commemorations identified in the *Lutheran Book of Worship*. Saints from every continent, every century, and every major Christian tradition are represented in this list of commemorations. It is edifying to remember them either on the day of their death or on the day of their commemoration, days which are often identical. A brief biography of each of the commemorated saints is available in the *Manual on the Liturgy*, a resource for use in connection with the *Lutheran Book of Worship*, or in *Festivals and Commemorations* by Philip H. Pfatteicher. Pfatteicher also provides readings by the saints, where available.

Another source of readings by the "cloud of witnesses" can be found in *For All the Saints*, a four-volume set of books for daily prayer edited by Frederick J. Schumacher. These are good and much-needed ways to confess this article of the Augsburg Confession.

Collect
Receive our thanks, dear God, for your countless saints, those known by the many, and those known only by a few. Your presence in their lives is a witness to your faithfulness. Their faith in you strengthens our faith. Their words and deeds inspire us to follow the one whom they followed, even Christ the Lord. Amen.

Congregational Prayer
Dear Lord, for all the saints we give you thanks. We are grateful that they ran the race despite the doubts and difficulties placed in their way by the enemy. Your constant care and limiting of Satan's evil won the day for them. You never gave them over to the evil one, even when they felt alone.

Our minds recall the lives of those in this congregation whom you have used as saints. Their steady work, their regular worship, their faith and their good deeds instill in us a joyful memory.

Help us imitate those who follow you. Fill us with the hope they receive from you, that this world is not the only world, and this experience is not the last experience, and the last word will be spoken by you at the end of time.

Bring us to read the written words of those whom you have called. By their words, and the words written about them, increase our faith.

When we pray, we pray to you Lord Jesus, but we especially remember your mother, Mary, and John, who stood beneath the cross with her. We remember the women who discovered the empty tomb and the disciples who laid down their lives for you. We remember the saints who have placed all their trust in you.

Their numbers are legion, and you call us as you called them. We give you our praise and thanks for inviting us to follow. Amen.

Personal Prayer

Lord Jesus Christ, thank you for coming to me through the witness of saints who have preceded me in life, and for the witness of saints who are living the faith today. Without their words and encouragement, I would not be talking to you now.

Thank you for those who brought me to the baptismal font, and for those who brought them. Thank you for Sunday worship where your pilgrim people still gather to receive your body and blood for the journey.

Thank you for those giants in the faith who never flinched, and thank you for those who flinched but came back again to faith.

Thank you for your Word which has confronted me again and again with joy and sorrow. Thank you for kindness that has come when I needed it most, and for the stern Word when I was drifting away. Thank you for silencing the evil one, when I was no longer able to shut him up. Thank you for people who held their criticism and gave mercy instead.

Thank you, dear Lord, for using me though I am not worthy. Thank you for letting your Word accomplish that which you promised it would do.

Thank you for inviting me to follow. Amen.

CONCLUSION TO PART I

This is about the sum of our teaching. As can be seen, there is nothing here that departs from the Scriptures or the catholic church or the church of Rome, in so far as the ancient church is known to us from its writers. Since this is so, those who insist that our teachers are to be regarded as heretics judge too harshly. The whole dissension is concerned with a certain few abuses which have crept into the churches without proper authority.... Among us the ancient rites are for the most part diligently observed, for it is false and malicious to charge that all ceremonies and all old ordinances are abolished in our churches. But it has been a common complaint that certain abuses were connected with ordinary rites. Because these could not be approved with a good conscience, they have to some extent been corrected.

PART II

Articles About Matters in Dispute
in Which an Account is Given of the Abuses
Which Have Been Corrected

*Inasmuch as our churches dissent from the church
catholic in no article of faith but only omit some few
abuses which are new and have been adopted by the fault
of the times although contrary to the intent of the canons
[decrees of councils], we pray that Your Imperial
Majesty will graciously hear both what has been changed
and what our reasons for such changes are in order that
the people may not be compelled to observe these abuses
against their conscience.*

ARTICLE 22

Both Kinds
in the Sacrament

[On restoring the chalice to the laity in Holy Communion]
*Among us both kinds [bread and wine] are given to
laymen in the sacrament. The reason is that there is a
clear command and order of Christ, "Drink of it, all of
you" (Matt. 26:27). Concerning the chalice Christ here
commands with clear words that all should drink of it.*

*... Not a single canon [decree of a council] can be
found which requires the reception of only one kind.
Nobody knows when or through whom this custom of
receiving only one kind was introduced, although
Cardinal Cusanus mentions when the use was approved.
It is evident that such a custom, introduced contrary to
God's command and also contrary to the ancient canons,
is unjust. Accordingly it is not proper to burden the
consciences of those who desire to observe the sacrament
according to Christ's institution or to compel them to act
contrary to the arrangement of our Lord Christ.*

Readings from the New Testament

And they said to him, "Grant us to sit, one at your right hand and one at your left, in your glory." But Jesus said to them, "You do not know what you are asking. Are you able to drink the cup that I drink, or be baptized with the baptism that I am baptized with?" They replied, "We are able." Then Jesus said to them, "The cup that I drink you will drink; and with the baptism with which I am baptized, you will be baptized; but to sit at my right hand or at my left is not mine to grant, but it is for those for whom it has been prepared" (Mark 10:37–40).

And going a little farther, he threw himself on the ground and prayed that, if it were possible, the hour might pass from him. He said, "Abba, Father, for you all things are possible; remove this cup from me; yet, not what I want, but what you want" (Mark 14:35–36).

Jesus said to Peter, "Put your sword back into its sheath. Am I not to drink the cup that the Father has given me?" (John 18:11).

Reflection

Let us not be deceived by some of the rhetoric used to defend this reform. Our Reformation ancestors were not claiming a right when they restored the chalice, the cup, to the laity in Holy Communion. They were determined to be obedient.

Obedience to Christ opens us to a promise of unspeakable comfort, for the great comforting promise of Christ is this: "Those who eat my flesh and drink my blood have eternal life, and I will raise them up on the last day; for my flesh is true food and my blood is true drink. Those who eat my flesh and drink my blood abide in me, and I in them" (John 6:54–56).

Obedience to Christ also opens us to a promise of unspeakable courage. The cup is not only the cup of the blood of Christ as the gift for eternal life. It is also the cup of Christ's courage to go to the cross, to offer up his life. What is more, he promises that it will be for our courage as well, the courage to offer our lives! "The cup that I drink you will drink," he says to James and John and to all of his disciples.

Christians no longer argue about whether both elements should be shared in the meal. Since the Second Vatican Council, the Roman Catholic Church permits the offering of wine to all communicants. So the first of the reform proposals that our Reformation ancestors made has ceased to be an issue that divides the parties involved in the Augsburg Confession.

What has become an issue in churches of the Augsburg Confession is whether we should continue the tradition of the common cup. We have grown accustomed to the wine. We have become fastidious about hygiene, concerned about germs. So we may not be as alert to the power in the sign of the common cup. We do not miss the power of the radical comfort, for the wine even in individual glasses conveys the great promise that when we drink his blood Christ abides in us and we in him. But we are in danger of missing Christ's promise that we will have the courage to drink *his* cup, that is, share in his offering, his mission, his suffering. And we are most in danger of missing the sign of unity involved in the common cup. Individual glasses cannot deprive us of the unity that Christ bestows in the meal. But they can deprive us of a sign that points to that unity.

Comfort and courage are the promises that Christ attaches to the cup of his precious blood. Faith clings to these promises even when our practices sometimes fall short of signaling their full power.

Collect

Lord Jesus Christ, do not let us pretend that we have glory like you, because you offer us your cup of suffering in the Holy Communion to drink. Fill us, instead, with gentleness of spirit, patience in suffering, and a willingness to be identified with the cross-lived life. Amen.

Congregational Prayer

Lord Jesus Christ, we confess that we too often come to the Holy Meal without discerning your presence. We drink your blood and eat your flesh, without remembering the cost of our own salvation.

We also confess, Lord Jesus Christ, that we seldom think of your presence at your table as the presence of eternal life. We forget that you have said that you will raise us up to eternal life.

Turn our minds and hearts away from the obvious unworthiness of our lives, to the great work you are doing in us, by feeding us yourself in the forms of bread and wine. Turn our minds to the gift you give us, that we may live this day full of confidence in the future, because you feed us your body and blood.

We remember your words: "I am the bread of life." We remember your promise, that once we drink of you we will not thirst again. Make us hungry and thirsty, famished and parched for you, that when you come to grace us with your presence, we may eat heartily and drink gladly from the plate and cup you extend. Amen.

Personal Prayer

Lord Jesus, I know many of your commands and many of your promises, but it is hard for me to make connections between the two. You command me to drink, and you promise me that if I drink of you I will thirst no more. You command me to love, and promise me that God is love. You command me to forgive, and promise me that you have already forgiven me.

It is in giving that you teach me to receive, I think, because you want me to know how the heavenly Father works. You want me to know what you know, that anything earned is less than that which is received as mercy, gift, or love.

I can admit to some unworthiness, Lord—a little. But you want my unworthiness known to me in depth. It feels like you want my blood, my pride, my sense of accomplishment. It feels like you want me poured out, like you were, on the cross, totally helpless and dependent upon grace, dependent upon God the Father for resurrection.

Raise me up, Lord, even now, from futile pride and strength. I do need your cup of salvation. I do ask you to do it your way. I do ask that I may rest in your promises, even when my patience and my sight are short. Amen.

ARTICLE 23

The Marriage of Priests

[On the reform of required celibacy for the clergy]

Among all people, both of high and of low degree, there has been loud complaint throughout the world concerning the flagrant immorality and the dissolute life of priests who were not able to remain continent and who went so far as to engage in abominable vices. In order to avoid such unbecoming offense, adultery, and other lechery, some of our priests have entered the married state....

It can be demonstrated from history and from the writings of the Fathers that it was customary for priests and deacons to marry in the Christian church of former times ...

...[I]n these last times of which the Scriptures prophesy, the world is growing worse and men are becoming weaker and more infirm.

Therefore it is most necessary, profitable, and Christian to recognize this fact in order that the prohibition of marriage may not cause worse and more disgraceful lewdness and vice to prevail in German lands. No one is able to alter or arrange such matters in a better or wiser way than God himself, who instituted marriage to aid human infirmity and prevent unchastity....

...[I]n the Holy Scriptures God commanded that marriage be held in honor. Marriage has also been highly praised in the imperial laws and in all states in which there have been laws and justice.

Readings from the New Testament

Now as an elder myself and a witness of the sufferings of Christ, as well as one who shares in the glory to be revealed, I exhort the elders among you to tend the flock of God that is in your charge, exercising the oversight, not under compulsion but willingly, as God would have you do it—not for sordid gain but eagerly. Do not lord it over those in your charge, but be examples to the flock (1 Peter 5:1–3).

The saying is sure: whoever aspires to the office of bishop desires a noble task. Now a bishop must be above reproach, married only once, temperate, sensible, respectable, hospitable, an apt teacher, not a drunkard, not violent but gentle, not quarrelsome, and not a lover of money (1 Timothy 3:1–3).

Reflection

At first glance this reform proposal seems to voice some of our anger and complaint as well. We do not have to read between the lines to note that our Reformation ancestors, too, were addressing an issue that makes headlines today. Pastors and bishops were betraying their office, transgressing sexual boundaries, sexually abusing their parishioners. And probably few of us think that clergy marriage is the appropriate remedy. "The world is growing worse," this article says. "Tell us about it!" we want to respond. But the challenge of this article is to hear a call of God that can transcend our disappointment or occasional outrage in some clergy and transform our cynicism about the state of marriage in general.

The clergy need our prayers, of course. What is more, they need a climate that supports their ministry as a calling from God, not a job as CEO of a religious business. Their calling to be "examples to the flock" means that they are to lead all Christians in lives that witness to God's vision for humanity. This is especially urgent if we are to obey God's command "that marriage be held in honor."

Our concerns today would probably be somewhat different than those of this article. On the basis of our experience, we would say that the church today needs ministry to marriage more than it needs marriage for ministers. The assaults of contemporary culture on marriage, home, and family are relentless. But God's command to honor marriage does not leave us without the resources of grace to support and sustain all who answer the call to make the commitment of marriage.

Collect

In your wisdom, Heavenly Father, you created us male and female, and gave us the gift of marriage, knowing that it is not good for us to be alone. Bless our relationships that we may find joy in one another, and give you thanks for all our family. Amen.

Congregational Prayer

Lord God, we come together as a family of faith, giving thanks for the gift of love that creates, through us, your children for the years to come.

Those of us who are married ask you to help us be faithful to our spouse, that your good gift of partnership will be an example to all, and pleasing to you.

Those of us who are single ask you for the gift of fidelity, and we give you thanks for our extended families.

Those of us who have experienced divorce rely on your mercy for the future, even as you grant forgiveness for the past.

All of us, Lord God, depend upon your joyful presence in our homes. We recommit ourselves to those whom we love that you have placed in our lives, and we give you thanks for those who love us, despite our shortcomings. Amen.

Personal Prayer

Lord God, do not let me yield to temptation in any way that dishonors your will for me or my home. I do not want to displease you, and I do not want to injure the ones you've given me as family.

The society, Lord, thinks your way is silly and the daily message of the media mocks you. Many friends tempt me to doubt the value of faithfulness and commitment. At times it seems as though all the world is saying, "It doesn't matter."

You matter, Lord. Your faithfulness to me matters immensely. You are clear in your expectations of me and generous in your gifts to me. You tell me clearly that my relationships are holy, and my family is precious. You give me courage to make a promise of fidelity, and the strength to keep it.

As you transform my will to one of joyful commitment, transform also the will of this society. May you be known as the only good that matters, and the only future available for humankind. Amen.

The Mass

[On the reform of the Holy Eucharist]

We are unjustly accused of having abolished the Mass. Without boasting, it is manifest that the Mass is observed among us with greater devotion and more earnestness than among our opponents. Moreover, the people are instructed often and with great diligence concerning the holy sacrament, why it was instituted, and how it is to be used ... in order that the people may be drawn to the Communion and Mass.... Meanwhile no conspicuous changes have been made in the public ceremonies of the Mass.... After all, the chief purpose of all ceremonies is to teach the people what they need to know about Christ....

Inasmuch, then, as the Mass is ... a Communion in which the priest and others receive the sacrament for themselves, it is observed among us in the following manner: On holy days [Sundays and festivals], and at other times when communicants are present [weekdays], Mass is held and those who desire it are communicated. Thus the Mass is preserved among us in its proper use.

Readings from the New Testament

While they were eating, Jesus took a loaf of bread, and after blessing it he broke it, gave it to the disciples, and said, "Take eat; this is my body." Then he took a cup, and after giving thanks he gave it to them, saying, "Drink from it, all of you; for this is my blood of the covenant, which is poured out for many for the forgiveness of sins. I tell you, I will never again drink of this fruit of the vine until that day when I drink it new with you in my Father's kingdom" (Matthew 26:26–29).

They devoted themselves to the apostles' teaching and fellowship, to the breaking of bread and the prayers (Acts 2:42).

Reflection

Our Reformation ancestors had such a clear agenda for the reform of the liturgy: Continue to do the Holy Communion, the Mass, every Sunday and every festival, but let it be the meal of the Gospel. It is a meal of the Gospel when we hear that the Father's kingdom has come in the death and resurrection of the Son, when we eat and drink it new with thanksgiving in the power of the Holy Spirit.

"Mass" means "mission," for it comes from the final Latin words of the liturgy, "*Ite, missa est.*" "Go, it is the sending!" The Sacrament was given to us as a meal, the "feast of victory for our God." The meal was given to us so that we would eat and drink and be sent into the world as the Body of Christ, set free to give ourselves for the life of the world.

Collect

Almighty God, before you send us out to do your work, you feed us with the body and blood of your Son, Jesus Christ. We receive him with thanksgiving, knowing that mercy and truth, righteousness and peace accompany us through your Holy Spirit. Amen.

Congregational Prayer

Lord God, Jesus loved the world in which we live, just like you. In the eating of this Holy Meal, O God, we recognize the need of the whole world. We also recognize the mission your Son, Jesus Christ, gives us in the world.

Jesus, you loved the world to which you were sent. Help us love it too, rightly, like you. Now, send us as ambassadors of your real presence. Send us, as God sent you, out of love for the world.

We ask that the bread and wine of the Eucharist fill us full of confidence, dear Lord, for it is your body and blood. Fill us full with thanksgiving, for you have given us a holy ministry, through grace, to a world lost in sin and selfishness. Help us give what we have received—relief of guilt from the past, and release from fear of the future.

Now, Lord God, give us confidence for this day and the week that is coming, for your Son is within and around us, ever present, always faithful, ever filled with grace enough for all.

As he sends us joyfully, so may we go joyfully, and be about your work, our Heavenly Father. Amen.

Personal Prayer

Dear Jesus, the sacrament of love always calls me to share in the world's heartache. It does me little good, and the world even less good, to complain and list the evils surrounding us all, for your arms are bigger, and your love is greater, and your will is stronger than all that confronts me every day.

Your example, Jesus, is so painful and powerful. It causes me to pull back in alarm. The world hurt you badly. Your love was rejected. You make it plain that it is real body and real blood in the Eucharist, not make-believe. I need courage, Lord Jesus, beyond the normal amount granted to a human being. I need your presence to be visible. I need to hear your Word ringing in my ears. I need your taste in my mouth, and your body feeding mine. I need more than an example. I need you.

All this you give, without my asking, but I ask, now, that I become acutely aware of your work through me, around me, and in spite of me, without ever rejecting me. I need the grace, Lord Jesus, I seek to share. I need the gift you give. Thank you. Amen.

ARTICLE 25

Confession

[On the reform of individual confession]
Confession has not been abolished by the preachers on our side.... At the same time the people are carefully instructed concerning the consolation of the Word of absolution so that they may esteem absolution as a great and precious thing. It is not the voice or word of the man who speaks it, but it is the Word of God, who forgives sin, for it is spoken in God's stead and by God's command.... We also teach that God requires us to believe this absolution as much as if we heard God's voice from heaven, that we should joyfully comfort ourselves with absolution, and that we should know that through such faith we obtain forgiveness of sins.

A Reading from the New Testament

[Jesus] entered Jericho and was passing through it. A man was there named Zacchaeus; he was a chief tax collector and was rich. He was trying to see who Jesus was, but on account of the crowd he could not, because he was short in stature. So he ran ahead and climbed a sycamore tree to see him, because he was going to pass that way. When Jesus came to the place, he looked up and said to him, "Zacchaeus, hurry and come down; for I must stay at your house today." So he hurried down and was happy to welcome him. All who saw it began to grumble and said, "He has gone to be the guest of one who is a sinner." Zacchaeus stood there and said to the Lord, "Look, half of my possessions, Lord, I will give to the poor; and if I have defrauded anyone of anything, I will pay back four times as much." Then Jesus said to him, "Today salvation has come to this house, because he too is a son of Abraham. For the Son of Man came to seek out and to save the lost" (Luke 19:1–10).

Reflection

The reform of the ritual of confessing our sins puts the emphasis where it belongs: on the forgiveness of sins and its liberating power. We do not confess in order to be forgiven. We are forgiven in order that we may be set free to confess. Sin burdens us in one of two ways.

The first way is that we do not trust God's forgiveness, and so we dare not be sinners. We cannot acknowledge that we have sinned. We just defend ourselves against every accusation, justify ourselves in every situation. The crucial point is that we must never appear to be in the wrong. Of course, this is an illusion, but we are driven to fool ourselves, even though we can't fool anyone else.

The second way is that we do not trust God's forgiveness, and so we despise ourselves; we despair because we are nothing but sinners. We have lost all of our defenses. We cannot affirm ourselves because we know that everyone sees through our excuses. Nothing can protect us from the contempt we are certain others must feel for us, for we hold ourselves in contempt.

Both ways in which sin burdens us can only be addressed by the Word of God's forgiveness. For when the Word of God says that we are forgiven, we dare to drop our defenses, to give up our self-justification. We dare to confess the truth about ourselves. The truth can be confessed and endured because it is not the last word about us. The last Word is: "You are forgiven." Because that is the last Word, we no longer need to despair. We can say YES to ourselves because in Christ the Triune God is saying YES to us. The Word of God in Christ is not "Maybe." In him it is always "Yes" (2 Corinthians 1:19). Zacchaeus heard that Word on the day that salvation came to his house in the person of Jesus.

Collect

Lord Jesus, may we hear your voice whenever the absolution is spoken, so that our sins, then removed, are removed forever, and we may joyfully begin our lives again, free and unencumbered by life-sapping guilt. Amen.

Congregational Prayer

Lord Jesus Christ, words of forgiveness were among the very last recorded words from your mouth. You were on the cross. You said, "Father, forgive them, because they do not know what they are doing."

No one asked you for it, but you gave forgiveness anyway. No one accepted it, at the moment, and the forgiveness seemed pointless. But when you came back from the dead, you showed your power over sin, death, and the devil, and now we know that when you say, "Your sins are forgiven," they are forgiven indeed. They are not just white-washed. They are sand-blasted away, by the same finger of God that wrote in the sand when Mary Magdalene stood before you, about to be stoned.

Lord Jesus Christ, keep us from doubting this power, and supposing that we need to continuously confess the same sins, over and over again. Once gone, they are gone forever. If brought back again and again, it is only a sign of our doubt, not your power.

Now, Lord Jesus Christ, as your children, washed by your forgiveness, give us courage to live a truly repentant life, by changing our behavior out of thanksgiving for your love. Amen.

Personal Prayer

Lord Jesus, help me replace my need for self-esteem with the more powerful and beautiful God-esteem, which you gave me when I was baptized and adopted as your child.

For too long I have defended myself, or accused myself. You only want me to give up myself into your care. You want me to trust you with my heart and my will, with my guilt and my shortcomings. You want my dreams, too, and my desire to be your person every day. To all of this you say, "Yes ...Yes, your sins are so far gone that I can no longer recall them myself. Yes, you are my child, forever, and you will never be abandoned by me. Yes, I can use you, even if all the strength you have left in you is a prayer. I will use you as my witness."

May I trust you, Lord Jesus, with all that is most precious to me—family, self, reputation, job, home, and life. Help me give thanks for all these gifts, but know that you surpass them all, for all came from you, and all can be restored when lost.

To you, O Lord, I give my thanks for forgiveness. May it work its joyous power within me. Amen.

ARTICLE 26

The Distinction of Foods

[On the reform of fasting]
In former times men taught, preached, and wrote that distinctions among foods and similar traditions which had been instituted by men serve to earn grace and make satisfaction for sin. For this reason new fasts, new ceremonies, new orders, and the like were invented daily, and were ardently and urgently promoted as if these were a necessary service of God by means of which grace would be earned if they were observed and a great sin committed if they were omitted. Many harmful errors in the church have resulted from this....

[Our teachers] have always taught concerning the holy cross that Christians are obliged to suffer, and this is true and real rather than invented mortification.

They also teach that everybody is under obligation to conduct himself, with reference to such bodily exercise as fasting and other discipline, so that he does not give occasion to sin, but not as if he earned grace by such works. Such bodily exercise should not be limited to

certain specified days but should be practiced con-
tinually.... Paul said that he pommeled his body and
subdued it, and by this he indicated that it is not the
purpose of mortification to merit grace but to keep the
body in such a condition that one can perform the duties
required by one's calling. Thus fasting in itself is not
rejected, but what is rejected is making a necessary
service of fasts on prescribed days and with specified
foods, for this confuses consciences.

Readings from the New Testament

[Jesus] called the crowd with his disciples, and said to them, "If any want to become my followers, let them deny themselves and take up their cross and follow me. For those who want to save their life will lose it, and those who lose their life for my sake, and for the sake of the gospel, will save it" (Mark 8:34–35).

And whenever you fast, do not look dismal, like the hypocrites, for they disfigure their faces so as to show others that they are fasting. Truly I tell you, they have received their reward. But when you fast, put oil on your head and wash your face, so that your fasting may be seen not by others but by your Father who is in secret; and your Father who sees in secret will reward you (Matthew 6:16–18).

Reflection

Most Christians today do not practice the discipline of fasting, except perhaps for giving up something during

Lent. This reform proposal no longer divides the Christian traditions involved in the Augsburg Confession. How shall we attend to its concerns? Our culture today challenges us to lose weight and eat correctly in order to have better bodily health. This can point us to appropriate reflection on this article.

Our Reformation ancestors regarded "such bodily exercise as fasting and other disciplines" as good and godly, not because they merit grace, but because they are expressions of faithful stewardship of the creation. God has entrusted the world to us, we are God's partners in the care of creation. In our time we are being warned by serious voices like the "World Watch Institute" that our current stewardship of the world threatens its future viability for our children and our grandchildren. The 1990 report of the institute seeks to help us envision a sustainable society, "one that satisfies its needs without jeopardizing the prospects of future generations. Inherent in this definition is the responsibility of each generation to ensure that the next one inherits an undiminished natural and economic endowment" (Brown 173).

Our Reformation ancestors have bequeathed to us a theological vision that affirms the world. It is God's good gift to us. With that gift comes responsibility. "In a world whose life is gravely jeopardized, the vocation to which Christians are called is the stewardship of life," wrote Douglas John Hall (68).

The call of God that we be faithful stewards is a sign of God's *trust* in humanity! Ponder this adaptation of a moving statement by Dutch theologian Edward

Schillebeeckx. "Despite everything, God never despairs of [humanity]. This is the [message of the creation narrative.] ... God trusts [humanity] to recreate *shalom* and order, salvation from and for [humanity], out of the chaos of our history. That is why the blessing of creation has been given to [human beings] by God through his royal and sovereign decree. God's trust is greater than all human failure. His kingdom is coming and one day will be inaugurated. God continues to trust [humankind]" (Schillebeeckx 109).

Collect

Lord God, protect us from a theology of glory that pretends a constant reward from you for our supposed faithfulness, making everything all right, everything fine. Protect us too, from a theology of despair, where there is no hope. Lead us to Christ, and the theology of the cross, where you work your will through us in joy and in suffering, in knowledge, and in God-given wisdom. Amen.

Congregational Prayer

Lord Jesus Christ, the invitation to "lose our lives for your sake" is frightful, if not impossible. Even when you add the promise that if we lose our lives for your sake, we "save" our lives, we are not ready to lose our whole life—maybe just the parts of it that pain us.

You, dear God, have never been known for understatement. You don't want just bits and dabs of us. You want all of every one of us. Do you want too much?

We would have to say "Yes, Lord," if it were anyone but you asking for so much. We would have to say "Yes, Lord," if we had done it and regretted it. We would have to say "Yes, Lord, you ask too much," if you weren't giving us more in return.

We know our lives need redeeming, Lord Jesus, and we invite you to lead us as you will into the total surrender of our lives for your sake, not just that we may be saved, though we yearn for that mightily, but simply because you are who you are, the Lord of all time, circumstance, and being. You, alone, know the full power and joy of a life of love. Amen.

Personal Prayer

Heavenly Father, seer in secret, keep me from pretending to a devotion I do not have. You cannot be fooled, even if I succeed in fooling others or myself. You do not take note of my pretenses, but only of my heart.

Dear God, seer in secret, keep me praying. You make my prayer real. You make it honest. You keep reminding me of the cross, and the way Jesus carried his. You invite me to let the yoke I bear be lifted by Christ, so that he might bear it with me. I keep asking you to take the burden away. Instead, you keep your Son trudging along beside me beneath the yoke.

For reasons I will never fully understand, dear God, you require labor where I would seek ease, and faith where I think I could go it alone. When I am ready for despair, you give hope, and when I think that the mountaintop has been gained, you show the possibility of a more glorious view ahead. I keep hoping that the next hill is not named Golgotha or Calvary. But you make no promise, except to be with me, beneath the yoke.

What wonderful company you are. How much easier the yoke is with you. Amen.

ARTICLE 27

Monastic Vows

[On the reform of Christian vocation]
In the days of St. Augustine monastic life was voluntary. Later, when true discipline and doctrine had become corrupted, monastic vows were invented, and the attempt was made to restore discipline by means of these vows as if in a well-conceived prison.

In addition to monastic vows many other requirements were imposed, and such fetters and burdens were laid on many before they had attained an appropriate age....

It was claimed that monastic vows were equal to Baptism, and that by monastic life one could earn forgiveness of sin and justification before God....

[I]t is taught among us with regard to those who desire to marry that all those who are not suited for celibacy have the power, right, and authority to marry, for vows cannot nullify God's order and command....

[T]he commands of God and true and proper service of God are obscured when people are told that monks alone are in a state of perfection. For this is Christian

perfection: that we fear God honestly with our whole
hearts, and yet have sincere confidence, faith, and trust
that for Christ's sake we have a gracious, merciful God;
that we may and should ask and pray God for those
things of which we have need, and confidently expect
help from him in every affliction connected with our
particular calling and station in life; and that meanwhile
we do good works for others and diligently attend to our
calling.

A Reading from the New Testament

I appeal to you therefore, brothers and sisters, by the
mercies of God, to present your bodies as a living
sacrifice, holy and acceptable to God, which is your
spiritual worship. Do not be conformed to this world,
but be transformed by the renewing of your minds, so
that you may discern what is the will of God—what is
good and acceptable and perfect (Romans 12:1–2).

Reflection

Our Reformation ancestors taught a great biblical
truth: All Christians belong to a holy priesthood by
virtue of their Baptism. Our baptismal priesthood
means three things.

First, we are priests when we gather to do the
Sunday liturgy. Our pastors preside over *our* liturgy,
but the liturgy belongs to us. It is what we have come to
do. For "liturgy" means "the work of the people." In
our liturgy we want to hear lessons from the Holy

Scripture. We want our pastors to preach the Word of God to us. We want to confess our faith, sing our praises to God, lay our needs and challenges before God in prayer, and offer ourselves into God's service. We want to share in the meal of Christ's body and blood, be taken up into Christ's body, and we want to be sent as Christ's body into the world.

Second, we are priests when we live our lives as callings, vocations, from God. This is one of the greatest gifts of the Lutheran reforms. We do not need to enter monasteries in order to serve God completely and fully. We are called by God to serve the coming of the kingdom of God through all the vocations of our daily life. We are called by God to serve peace and justice, to serve the good order and the fruitfulness of the world, to serve all of humanity with compassion and care.

Third, we are priests when we say our daily prayers and commend ourselves and our world to God. True spiritual priesthood means giving yourself to God for your neighbor's sake, not giving yourselves to your neighbor for God's sake. Christian prayer does not mean bringing your concerns to God. It means finding yourself in the heart of God, and then discovering what is in God's heart for you and for others.

Collect

Lord God, teach us. Teach us to live in this world, knowing that our time here is full of divine purpose. Teach us to love in this world, that the earth and the cosmos may be transformed, through the renewal of our minds in Christ Jesus. Amen.

Congregational Prayer

Heavenly Father, be with us in our worship this day, as we receive your grace to serve you in the world. Be with us when we return to our separate vocations, that we may be your person in our daily work, as well as in our weekly worship. Be with us in our daily prayers, too, that we may become your person at all times and in all places.

We give you thanks for using us as your hands, feet, voice, ears, and mind. Teach us to dare not touch any work without your prodding, go anywhere where we would not be proud to have you alongside, speak no word but what would be pleasing to your ears, listen to no voice that would shame us in your presence, and think no thoughts that would cause you injury.

We give you thanks for using us. May all our good works be no less, and no more, than a simple thank-you for all your goodness toward us.

Now transform us. Through the mind of Christ, transform us. Let his way become so well known to us, that his way will be lived naturally by us. Amen.

Personal Prayer

Lord God, sometimes I think I work too hard trying to please you. Sometimes I imagine that you require more of me than what I am, or have, or ought to become. Sometimes I still try to earn your love and salvation. I note the sacrifices and lives of the saints before me, and marvel at their devotion. I would be like them, if only I could.

Help me look at the gifts you have given me as special—so special that no one else has ever been called to go to the places I can go, be with the people I can be with, and do the things that you've equipped me to do over the years. Keep me from coveting anyone else, whether in love, or service, or skill, or recognition of service in your kingdom. Help me be content with my calling, and not to desire my sister's or brother's calling.

Transform my mind, Lord Jesus, so that my life is no attempt to prove its value to you or to myself. Transform my life, that I may rest entirely confident, that when my life comes to completion in this world, it will be resumed in the next, by your power, out of your goodness, and for purposes known only to you. Amen.

ARTICLE 28

The Power of Bishops

[On the reform of the ministry of bishops]
Our teachers assert according to the Gospel the power of keys or the power of bishops is a power and command of God to preach the Gospel, to forgive and retain sins, and to administer and distribute the sacraments....

This power of keys or of bishops is used and exercised only by teaching and preaching the Word of God and by administering the sacraments (to many persons or to individuals, depending on one's calling). In this way are imparted not bodily but eternal things and gifts, namely, eternal righteousness, the Holy Spirit, and eternal life.... Inasmuch as the power of the church or of bishops bestows eternal gifts and is used and exercised only through the office of preaching, it does not interfere at all with government or temporal authority. Temporal authority is concerned with matters altogether different from the Gospel. Temporal power does not protect the soul, but with the sword and physical penalties it protects body and goods from the power of others....

Thus our teachers distinguish the two authorities and the functions of the two powers, directing that both be held in honor as the highest gifts of God on earth....

According to divine right, therefore, it is the office of the bishop to preach the Gospel, forgive sins, judge doctrine and condemn doctrine that is contrary to the Gospel, and exclude from the Christian community the ungodly whose wicked conduct is manifest. All this is to be done not by human power but by God's Word alone. On this account parish ministers and churches are bound to be obedient to the bishops according to the saying of Christ in Luke 10:16, "He who hears you hears me."...

[St.] Peter forbids the bishops to be domineering and to coerce the churches. It is not our intention that the bishops give up their power to govern, but we ask for this one thing, that they allow the Gospel to be taught purely and that they relax some few observances which cannot be kept without sin. If they are unwilling to do this and ignore our petition, let them consider how they will answer for it in God's sight, inasmuch as by their obstinacy they offer occasion for division and schism, which they should in truth help to prevent.

A Reading from the New Testament

When they had finished breakfast, Jesus said to Simon Peter, "Simon son of John, do you love me more than these?" He said to him, "Yes, Lord; you know that I love you." Jesus said to him, "Feed my lambs." A second time he said to him, "Simon son of John, do you love me?" He said to him, "Yes Lord; you know that I love you." Jesus said to him, "Tend my sheep." He said to him the third time, "Simon son of John, do you love me?" Peter felt hurt because he said to him the third time, "Do you love me?" And he said to him, "Lord, you know everything; you know that I love you." Jesus said to him, "Feed my sheep" (John 21:15–17).

A Reading from the Old Testament

Therefore, you shepherds, hear the word of the Lord: As I live, says the Lord God, because my sheep have become a prey, and my sheep have become food for all the wild animals, since there was no shepherd; and because my shepherds have not searched for my sheep, but the shepherds have fed themselves, and have not fed my sheep; therefore, you shepherds, hear the word of the Lord: Thus says the Lord God, I am against the shepherds; and I will demand my sheep at their hand, and put a stop to their feeding the sheep; no longer shall the shepherds feed themselves....

I myself will be the shepherd of my sheep, and I will make them lie down, says the Lord God. I will seek the lost, and I will bring back the strayed, and I will bind up the injured, and I will strengthen the weak, but the fat and the strong I will destroy. I will feed them with justice (Ezekiel 34:7–10; 15–16).

Reflection

This is the longest article in the Augsburg Confession, and, even though it was the last article read to the emperor, it was, according to scholars, the first one written. Its length and its importance point to the deep problem confronting our Reformation ancestors: leadership in the church. Secular scholars as well as church historians have noted that pastoral leadership in Germany and Italy at the time of the Lutheran Reformation was at one of the lowest points in Christian history. In spite of that, our Reformation ancestors pledged obedience also to bad bishops if only the preaching of the Gospel and these modest reforms would be permitted.

What is more important for us is the vision of good bishops contained in this article. In the United States, only the Evangelical Lutheran Church in America (ELCA) has adopted the title "bishop" to describe its regional leaders, each of whom is called to be a "pastor of pastors." Other Lutheran churches may use other ways of referring to this office. Nevertheless, the call is the same. They are to care for the church by preaching the Gospel, administering the sacraments, attending to the purity of the Gospel by condemning what is contrary to it and warning the church, being concerned about sinners and admonishing them. We need to seek out persons for the office of bishop who can give such leadership to the church. We need to pray always for our leaders that they be such bishops. We need to give thanks to God when we are given such bishops.

Collect

Strengthen, Lord Jesus, the pastors and bishops of your church, that they may be led by your Holy Spirit to preach the Gospel with conviction, absolve sinners with mercy, and administer the sacraments with joy and thanksgiving. Amen.

Congregational Prayer

Lord Jesus Christ, we give you thanks for calling some to positions of leadership in the church. Help us support them in their duties, pray for them by name, learn from their teaching and preaching, and accept their spoken absolution to our confession of sin as though the forgiveness came directly from your mouth.

We remember the admonition given to Peter at the seashore after your resurrection: "Feed my sheep." Keep us from being surprised if you counsel us as you did Peter. May we have Peter's grace to accept your questioning word and admonition as forgiveness, taking comfort that we are still of much value to you and your work.

Lord Jesus, give us the gift of your Holy Spirit, that we may be most concerned about eternal matters. May we live as though our current life is not to be compared in value to the life that is coming. May we seek to be fed as sheep of your flock, and to feed others as duty and opportunity occur, that we may be both faithful followers and wise leaders.

At all times, protect us from the desire for earthly power, but give us courage in times of judgment and authority that you assign us, that your will may be done. Amen.

Personal Prayer

As a leader in your church, Lord God, help me to fathom and give thanks for your love of the poor, the weak, the injured, and the lost. I am one of them more often than I am your bold leader. I need a shepherd too. I need the searching eye, the caring word, the gentle understanding, the corrective advice, and the supporting hand that only you can give.

You come to me as a shepherd, Lord Jesus, through other shepherds. You make me need others. You let me see you in the lives of your followers. Your light shines brightly on me in the kind acts of my sisters and brothers. You don't counsel me from a distance. You come to me with human feet and words.

Sometimes I have wanted more ... something like an angel or a personal audience with you. Sometimes I thought you were distant, but when I remember your ways, my eyes are opened, and my ears are unstopped. You make me look and listen. You make me notice the person coming into my life, sent by you, shepherding.

What a Good Shepherd, you are, Lord Jesus, with uncounted thousands of under-shepherds doing your work. Thank you for letting me be one of them. Thank you for every one of them who has ever come to me. Thank you. Amen.

CONCLUSION

These are the chief articles that are regarded as controversial....

It must not be thought that anything has been said or introduced out of hatred or for the purpose of injuring anybody, but we have related only matters which we have considered it necessary to adduce and mention in order that it may be made very clear that we have introduced nothing, either in doctrine or ceremonies, that is contrary to Holy Scripture or the universal Christian church. For it is manifest and evident (to speak without boasting) that we have diligently and with God's help prevented any new and godless teaching from creeping into our churches and gaining the upper hand in them.

In keeping with the summons, we have desired to present the above articles as a declaration of our confession and the teaching of our preachers. If anyone should consider that it is lacking in some respect, we are ready to present further information on the basis of the divine Holy Scripture.

Your Imperial Majesty's most obedient servants:
JOHN, duke of Saxony, elector
GEORGE, margrave of Brandenburg
ERNEST, duke of Lüneburg
PHILIP, landgrave of Hesse

JOHN FREDERICK, duke of Saxony
FRANCIS, duke of Lüneburg
WOLFGANG, prince of Anhalt
Mayor and council of Nuremberg
Mayor and council of Reutlingen

A Reading from the New Testament

Come to [Christ], a living stone, though rejected by mortals yet chosen and precious in God's sight, and like living stones, let yourselves be built into a spiritual house, to be a holy priesthood, to offer spiritual sacrifices acceptable to God through Jesus Christ....

[For] you are a chosen race, a royal priesthood, a holy nation, God's own people, in order that you may proclaim the mighty acts of him who called you out of darkness into his marvelous light....

Beloved, I urge you as aliens and exiles to abstain from the desires of the flesh that wage war against the soul. Conduct yourselves honorably among the Gentiles, so that, though they malign you as evildoers, they may see your honorable deeds and glorify God when he comes to judge.

For the Lord's sake accept the authority of every human institution, whether of the emperor as supreme, or of governors, as sent by him.... As servants of God, live as free people, yet do not use your freedom as a pretext for evil. Honor everyone. Love the family of believers. Fear God. Honor the emperor (1 Peter 2:4–5; 9; 11–14; 16–17).

Reflection

The signatures of these laymen—and they were all men at that time in the church's history—should still move us to awe and gratitude. Of course they listened to their theologians; of course they asked Philip Melanchthon to write their confession. But in a highly charged and very dangerous situation, with their lives at stake, they were willing to take responsibility for the confession of the Christian Gospel. They were willing to seek the renewal and reform of the church in German states and cities. They had to know enough to decide that this was worth risking their jobs, to say nothing of their lives.

"The church" is not its theologians and teachers, not its bishops and pastors, not its deacons and lay employees. The church is its people. Of course the people must learn from the teaching of the theologians, ponder the initiatives of bishops and other leaders, welcome the preaching and sacramental presidency of pastors, benefit from the ministry of all persons whom the church employs. But, most importantly, the people must care about the integrity of the Gospel, take ownership for the administration of the sacraments, and be Christ's witnesses in the world both individually and corporately.

In Germany four centuries after the laymen made their confession at Augsburg, lay men and women were leaders in the "confessing church" as it brought its witness against the Nazi regime. Among the great members of the "confessing church" to offer up their lives as witnesses and confessors of the Gospel were leaders of the German nobility like Count Helmuth von

Moltke. When he was sentenced to death, the Nazi judge, Roland Freisler, said, "Count Moltke, Christianity and we National Socialists have one thing in common, and one thing only: we claim the whole man."

Indeed. The Gospel claims men and women wholly, and Christ's unbreakable promise is that life, not death, will have the last word! When the people of the church believe that good news, they become witnesses and confessors.

A Closing Prayer

You claim us, Almighty God, in the name of the Father who created us, in the name of the Spirit who visits us, and in the name of the Son who died for us.

You have given everything. No saint has matched it. No poet could devise such a love. No theologian has ever been able to thoroughly describe it. No pastor can preach it perfectly. No ear can hear the whole marvel.

You are beyond confession and comprehension. Earth, sea, and sky cannot contain you. Eternity is your routine experience. History is the record of your faithfulness. Time, light, and love are your hand tools. Death is no more. And we, dear God, are the objects of your love and affection, made in your image, with the invisible capacities to trust, to hope, and to love.

We wait for the day of resurrection, and we look forward to the world that is coming. Give us the courage to finish the work you have assigned for humankind to accomplish, and, when the time is right, come, Lord Jesus, come. Amen.

WORKS CITED

Berdiaev, Nikolai, *Spirit and Reality*, G. Bles, London (1946).

Brown, Lester R., Flavin, Christopher, and Postel, Sandra, "Picturing a Sustainable Society," *State of the World, 1990*, W. W. Norton & Company, New York (1990).

Hall, Douglas John, *The Stewardship of Life in the Kingdom of Death*, Friendship Press, New York (1985).

Luther, Martin, "The Large Catechism," *The Book of Concord: The Confessions of the Evangelical Lutheran Church*, T. G. Tappert, Editor, Fortress Press, Philadelphia, PA (1959).

Luther, Martin, Sermon on Indulgences, February 24, 1517, "Sermons: I," Vol. 51, J. Doberstein, Editor, *Luther's Works* (American Edition), Fortress Press, Philadelphia, PA (1959).

Lutheran-Episcopal Dialogue, Series III, *Implications of the Gospel*, W. A. Norgren and W. G. Rusch, Editors, Augsburg Publishing House, Minneapolis, MN, Forward Movement Publications, Cincinnati, OH (1988). With study guide by D. J. Swan and E. Z. Turner.

Schillebeeckx, Edward, *Interim Report on the Books Jesus and Christ*, Crossroad Publishing Company, New York, (1981).

Soelle, Dorothee, *Suffering*, translation by E. R. Kalin, Fortress Press, Philadelphia, PA (1975).

OTHER WORKS MENTIONED

For All the Saints: A Prayer Book For and By the Church, Vol.s 1–4, F. J. Schumacher and D. A. Zelenko, Editors, American Lutheran Publicity Bureau, Delhi, NY (1994–1996).

Luther, Martin, "The Bondage of the Will," in *Martin Luther: Selections from His Writings*, J. Dillenberger, Editor, Doubleday & Co., Inc., New York (1958).

Lutheran Book of Worship, prepared by Inter-Lutheran Commission on Worship, Augsburg Publishing House, Minneapolis, MN, and Board of Publication, Lutheran Church in America, Philadelphia, PA (1978).

Pfatteicher, Philip H., and Messerli, Carlos R., *Manual on the Liturgy*, Augsburg Publishing House, Minneapolis, MN (1979).

Pfatteicher, Philip H., *Festivals and Commemorations*, Augsburg Publishing House, Minneapolis, MN (1980).

FOR FURTHER READING

Kolb, Robert, *Confessing the Faith: Reformers Define the Church, 1530–1580*, Concordia Publishing House, St. Louis, MO (1991).

Grane, Leif, *The Augsburg Confession: A Commentary*, translated by J. H. Rasmussen, Augsburg Publishing House, Minneapolis, MN (1987).

Gritsch, Eric W., and Jenson, Robert W., *Lutheranism: The Theological Movement and Its Confessional Writings*, Fortress Press, Philadelphia, PA (1976).

Mahsman, David L., *Augsburg Today—This We Believe, Teach, and Confess*, Concordia Publishing House, St. Louis, MO (1997).

ABOUT THE AUTHOR

Richard Bansemer has served Lutheran parishes in Florida, Colorado, and Virginia. In 1987 he was elected bishop of the Virginia Synod, Evangelical Lutheran Church in America. He is the author of several books of sermons and prayers. His recent book, *O Lord, Teach Me to Pray: A Catechetical Prayer Book for Personal Use*, is based on Luther's Small Catechism and is offered by The American Lutheran Publicity Bureau as a companion volume to *We Believe: A Prayer Book Based on the Augsburg Confession*.